T0021347

$¥ST€MS

Bibliography

Escobar, A. (2018) *Designs for the Pluriverse* (New Ecologies for the Twenty-First Century). Duke University Press.

Jenner, K. (2016) *Chill Kendall Jenner Didn't Think People Would Care That She Deleted Her Instagram*. In: *Vogue*. Available at: https://www.vogue.com/article/kendall-jenner-deletes-instagram-thought-no-one-would-care

Jurgenson, N. (2019) *On Photography and Social Media*. London: Verso Books.

Keedy, J. (2001) *Hysteria™ – Intelligent Design, Not Clever Advertising*. In: Heller, S. & Vienne, V. Eds. (2003) *Citizen Designer – Perspectives on Design Responsibility*. New York: Allworth Press, pp. 206–209.

Keedy, J. (1997) *Greasing the Wheels of Capitalism with Style and Taste, Or, The "Professionalization" of American Graphic Design*. In: Bierut, M.; Drenttel, W. & Heller, S. (2012) *Looking Closer 4: Critical Writings on Graphic Design*. Allworth Press, pp. 199–207.

Manzini, E. (2015) *Design, When Everybody Designs: An Introduction to Design for Social Innovation*. Massachusetts: MIT Press.

Meadows, D. (2008) *Thinking in Systems*. London: Earthscan.

Mouffe, C. (2009) *The Democratic Paradox*. London: Verso Books.

Mülller-Brockmann, J. (1981) *Grid Systems in Graphic Design: A Handbook for Graphic Artists, Typographers, and Exhibition Designers*. Niggli Verlag.

Smith, B. (1977) *Conceptual Design – A Polemic*. In: Bicknell, J. & McQuiston, L. Eds. (1977) *ICSID, Design For Need – The Social Contribution of Design*. London: Pergamon Press. pp. 108–115.

Graphic Design Systems, and the Systems of Graphic Design
Francisco Laranjo

Within graphic design, the concept of systems is profoundly rooted in form. When a term such as system is invoked, it is normally related to macro and micro-typography, involving book design and typesetting, but also addressing type design or parametric typefaces. Branding and signage are two other domains which nearly claim exclusivity of the use of the word 'systems' in relation to graphic design. A key example of this is the influential book *Grid Systems in Graphic Design* (1981) by Swiss designer Josef Müller-Brockmann. More than structures of organisation of form, this books shapes a mathematical, delusional and purist way of thinking. With the use of the grid as an ordering system, Müller-Brockmann argues that a "design which is objective, committed to the common weal, well composed and refined constitutes the basis of democratic behaviour." (Müller-Brockmann, 1981, p. 10) He makes a case for the universal validity of grid systems, claiming that the systematic use of strict formal principles produces directness and intelligibility, which he suggests are vital in sociopolitical life. This position is a political choice. One that is driven and enforced by form, rapidly reproducible and scalable, and with damaging consequences by his reductive definition of democracy. By letting mathematical form define democracy as a controlling system, Müller-Brockmann strives for neutrality and a common good. Such sweeping levelling overlooks privilege, under-representation, marginalisation, difference. It excludes plurality. Political theorist Chantal Mouffe (2009) argues that a pluralist democracy should legitimise conflict,

5

division, and antagonism. And for such democracy to exist, "no social agent should be able to claim any mastery of the foundation of society" (Mouffe, 2009, p. 21). In other words, Müller-Brockmann's system of organisation of form shapes a way of thinking—a consistent formal system at the cost of difference. His definition of systemic form reproduces a limited definition of democracy. The illusion of universality and objectivity coming from a specific historic and geopolitical context is exported worldwide to the present day and still applied with the same conviction, or simply as eternally marketable style, with multiple reincarnations. These are not design systems of universal validity. They are systems of oppressive deception.

Display Systems
Rita González, a design lecturer from Colombia, had only been teaching for three years when a series of circumstances, and some openness from senior management, promoted her to head of department. Despite likely finding structural opposition, she didn't lose time, unhappy with design education in the country and a toxic system that feeds an industry that invariably invests all the time polishing and displaying the surface. Rita knows social media hasn't radically changed designers' lives. But Instagram has changed graphic design forever. Launched in 2010, after Facebook and Twitter, Instagram developed and further potentiated a culture of display. For graphic design, it was love at first sight: an opportunity to merge the personal—even the intimate—with the professional and public through relentless, seductive, profitable, addictive, self-branding normality. What initially appeared to be a platform to share photos, revealed itself as a form of life, providing data and ad revenue to thousands of corporations, while designing designers before they even enter design education.

6

Through repetition and imposed fear of exclusion, branding is automatically taught to children from a young age, maximised by the use of mobile devices. Before reaching high school, students have have formed a conception of branding, particularly self-branding, influencing and shaping also all definitions of *identity*. It's all just a game. Playful. Enjoyable. Totalising. A never-ending cycle of branding, advertising and revenue-generation. Branding is gamification. Like the popular videogame *Fortnite*, Instagram is not a matter of sharing, displaying or gloating, but of survival.

When Instagram copied Snapchat's core functionality of posting temporary images and videos—a beaming live feed of a grand narrative—it massified personal reality shows. With this functionality, which is inherently built into to the platform's business model, Instagram's true achievement is making everyone believe in the singularity and originality of each of its users' *stories*. Instagram (read Facebook, its owner) effectively controls and shapes the desires and expectations of consumption through data management as a business system. Designers post what they eat, crop the photos, boost the colour levels and apply the most appropriate filter to make it look 'professional'—a meaningless word in the age of instant professionalism. Designers post what they bought, where they are going, where they were and are, providing revenue to invisible shareholders. Posing as design practice is inevitable.

On the first day of the term, Rita deactivated the Wi-Fi on campus—if students wanted to use internet, they would need to go to an Ethernet-connected computer in the library. A small gesture, she knows, but it would make a lot of people uncomfortable. The new 5G network had just been installed in Bogotá, despite protests against the refusal by local authorities to survey the risks to public health. Dark studio, students lit up their phone screens—there's no Wi-Fi—what's happening? With a serious tone, Rita introduced herself to the new class: "Not having Instagram is not existing. If it was not

7

posted, it never happened. Designers must follow friends out of loyalty and like acquaintances' posts out of courtesy. And PR. Always. One *like* is a window of opportunity, and no window can be left untapped. Accordingly, every time a designer is mentioned is an opportunity to broadcast that mention, the equivalent of a visual echo, which only social media allows with the kind of quantity and short time intervals our desire for attention demands. Social media capital is a relevance greeting card, a decision-making factor in our limited attention-span. To make things worse, graphic design is amnesiac. Instagram accelerates this to new levels. The discipline's capacity to remember history is proportional to our patience to scroll down or swipe up. We may get to see what has been tagged, suggested or related recently—properly categorised for algorithmic exploitation. The rest is forgotten, uncategorised, lost, data-less information that is immediately ignored and classified as trifling. Instagram provides designers comfort and anxiety in equal measure. Soothing, stunning, stressful." "Welcome everyone", she continued, "things are going to change around here!".

Ranking Systems

An Instagram video is trending: "I felt like—I just wanted a little bit of a break. I'm always on it. I feel I would wake up in the morning and I would look at it first thing. I would go to bed, and it was the last thing that I would look at. It just, I felt a little too dependent on it. I kind of wanted to take a minute; it's a detox. I'll be back! I'll come back.", said socialite Kendall Jenner to the TV Presenter Ellen DeGeneres in 2016. It's a lot of competition. And competition is synonym of design. Neri Smith, a graphic designer/ visual artist/ information architect knows this all too well.

　　She wakes up, barely opening her eyes and taps on Instagram: are there notifications? What's happening? It's 7am and there are already so many stories she's missing.

With effort, she checks a few: some friends, some partners, some colleagues, some jealousy. Her eyes begin to focus: "They did what? Oh, that's a nice photo! He's where? Soooo lucky." She can't believe it. It's enough to make her jump out of bed and quickly eat some mango yoghurt that was left in the fridge. Phone sitting next to her bowl, she swipes up, then a bit down, up again. It feels like checking the news, but better, somewhere between pleasure, teasing and sadness of what's going on in the world—some family, too—a good mix of what she likes to see. She curated her feed well, it's a lot of work, and it pays off. It's an investment in the future. Time for a quick bit of yoga.

A suggested account brightens up the screen: @dezeen? Follow. Three more show up next to it: @designboom, @digital_archive, @swissposters. Follow, follow, follow. It's time to take a shower and get dressed. Steamed bathroom, lavender smell, but it's still possible to see that notifications are appearing on the screen. It's too far to see what it is. The tap is turned off. It was just just @biennale.design.graphique that liked one of her photos and @itsnicethat that started a live feed—"got to turn off this thing"; Neri thought she did but it keeps appearing anyway. So annoying! Someone is tinkering with this, surely!

She's on her way to work. If it wasn't for Instagram, she would be bored to death. But she still is, although it doesn't feel like it. Swipe up, swipe up, down, stop, zoom in, and up again. New follower: @newstudiostudio, nice clean type, branding studio, possible future employer. Follow back. Another account is suggested: @thedesignblacklist. She reads the bio: "Minimalist detox. A curated collection of design inspiration." Photographed work with 45° angle, a good selection of printed stuff in black and white. And inspiration is always good. We can't have enough inspiration. Follow. Is she following too many people at 2,231K? Maybe it's a bit desperate, a bit embarrassing. She should unfollow a few accounts, do a clean up of

9

abandoned handles or things she doesn't like anymore. Below 2K would be cooler. Maybe later, not now. This constant pressure is so draining, it's like a design ranking race. We have design stars with more than 150K followers, the very famous with 20K+ followers, the established designers with 5–10K followers, the rising designers with 3–5K and all the rest with less than 1K, they're just not good enough. Seriously, who wants to succeed in design with less than 1K?

Toilet breaks are great to check Instagram. During work hours Neri is too busy to catch up with friends' stories, which drives her insane at times. And at work, it's not good to be always looking at her phone—even if discretely under the table during meetings. Wow, @jessicavwalsh just launched @andwalsh. The photos to kick-start the studio are cool, done in a photo studio and a good amount of Photoshop, polished, vivid, dramatic. Cats! @cats_of_instagram is a guilty pleasure. So is @uglydesign. Share. Send. @clippingsdesign? Why not? Follow. An email notification slides from the top down: it's from Social Digger, luring Neri into buying followers to grow her business and profile online. It's only $98 for 10K followers instead of the usual $115.99 USD. Tempting. And in her circle of friends, many are over 4K and she doesn't want to slip in their estimation. She wasn't paying attention and the meeting continued. Lunch break is here, a moment to swipe up and tap incessantly while the other hand holds the fork. The salad looks too good. A photo from the top will make sure her group of friends know she's living a healthy life and slowly enjoying her lunch break. Selects her favourite filter, increases the saturation and another 'moment' is uploaded to her story while geotagging the bar. The phone needs to be charged with just 54% battery left. Lunch is over, back to work.

Award Systems
Marielle Silva is a design student at the university where Rita González teaches. Every year, she has to participate in design

competitions as part of the curriculum. Her tutors say it's good for students to have an experience of the real world, with real deadlines and real jurors, experienced people with awards and successful studios who spend some time looking at what they've done. And that it's a shot at professional life—a contact, a reference, a mention, an email, perhaps even a job offer? Competition brief after brief, many students spend their whole education allured by awards, targeting medals and recognition by their peers, effectively nourishing a design ethos which reverberates across the discipline, mainly through social media, producing an inward-looking industry of disposable time, work, and citizenship. The following year there's always more.

Two awards fight for hegemony in design education: D&AD and the Red Dot Awards. These are followed by ISTD (International Society of Typographic Designers) and The Design Museum. Graphis and the European Design Awards are then joined by dozens of other trying to outshine each other, attract sponsorship, raise and push profiles in galas, award ceremonies and networking cocktails. To complement these, there are elite clubs such as AGI (Alliance Graphique Internationale), which despite AGI Open (a series of mainly portfolio talks by a selection of members) promote the kind of closed, inward-looking, swanky shoulder-rubbing get-togethers that many designers aspire to as a lifetime-achievement award, a yearned ticket to eternal design stardom. With expensive, glossy tomes spread on desks in the university's studio, it is no wonder Marielle is both distant but seduced by the publications produced every year by these institutions. Departments encourage and pay for students to participate in these competitions, displaying certificates on corridor walls as badges of merit. It is the feeding of a vicious system which sees academia merge with and be subservient to the market, corporations and institutional political interests.

In 2018, Marielle's group of friends chose the D&AD brief set by the sportswear brand Adidas in collaboration with H+K Strategies. The brief talked profusely about 'change' – a catchword in early 21st century – saying that Adidas "is driven by helping athletes make a difference in their game, their lives and the world." Rita is annoyed that this is still the dominant educational model at her university. And she is furious that, predictably, a brief like this adopts the typical capitalist approach of demanding that yet another product, brand service or campaign is created. Directed at a 17–25 age group, the brief asked "What can Adidas do for or with them to improve the fabric of their city?" This brief reinforces a design system that teaches students that social and political phenomena can only be addressed through a consumable, branded product, surveillance capitalism and submission to corporations. And nearly every project at school has at least one brand attached to it in some form. "It's not design education, it's *branducation*", said Rita in a recent departmental meeting. To Marielle, this is obvious in the wording of the brief: "Show how people will experience it, how it could scale and spread, and all the media, channels and touchpoints that could be relevant. What different social platforms or formats could you use, and how would content be tailored to each?" It continues: "Adidas wants to see big, bold ambition, clearly grounded in reality". The bouquet is complete with the following message: "Don't get political. Stay true to the brand tone of voice."

In that same year, Amazon equipped every classroom of her university with Alexa. The students did not feel too comfortable with an object always listening to what they say. But it was useful to order consumables and for the games of design trivia they played every once in a while, and for the lectures of design history. Marielle, Andrea, Pedro and Letizia were fed up with generic information, with Wikipedia lectures and lack of representation. Always the same references, always the same authors from the same places, the same canon,

12

always the same marginalisation. Together, they've hacked their studio's device and collectively built a new database and algorithms for the fellow students to see and edit. "What's an influencer?", they asked with a smirk. Alexa now replied: "Denomination used in the late 2010s to describe people who use social media as self-centred representation of click-capitalism, seeing every blink of an eye as an opportunity for mass consumerism." A strangely pitched sound followed: "Reminder: I'm built by schoolchildren in China" and "Attention, this product needs an official Amazon update, please return to factory settings and visit Amazon.com for details." The IT technicians would surely just ask senior management to ask for a replacement, but during any lunch break they could hack it again. However, their small but most meaningful gesture was to collectively mobilise themselves and force the school's management to remove all these devices from the classrooms.

Another group of friends chose a brief that aimed to address loneliness and elderly people. Marielle enjoyed the typographic illustrations of the campaign her friends did in response to the brief—typography that was slightly hard to read, twisted as if it was photocopied while gently moving the printed page. It was a variable font that aimed to convey depressive moods and isolation, with a coded application that allowed different parameters to generate multiple outputs. White type on black background, the large-scale posters filled metro stations in well-lit renders. They also made an app that allowed people to experience the poster in augmented reality, in which type would move, hypnotic as it was dropping out of the poster in an infinite loop and providing a phone number for people to seek help. Marielle thought it was impressive but useless. Why do posters in the first place? And an app, to elderly people? With fancy animated type? Why is design and all its typical production even needed? How much would this campaign cost?

13

Wouldn't the money be better spent in a community centre? Which institutions and people are already working on this for decades? Did they bother to learn? The posters were on brand, a cohesive visual language rolled out to multiple media. And that's the most important for the award juries. She knows this wouldn't even be questioned by them, lacking the nuanced, in-depth knowledge that would allow them to make politically and socially-informed judgments. It's irrelevant. What matters is the gold, silver and bronze for the amazing augmented reality. It will enter in the media echo chamber until the sound slowly fades. The future of design is not being built by sharing or cooperation or solidarity, but competition. By outrunning, outshining and outburning each other.

Alternative Systems

The seduction of systematic form, constant production, social media showcasing and competition sustain the infrastructure that defines graphic design. It shapes an industry that thrives in auto-pilot towards self-destruction, surrendered to the economic system in which it operates: capitalism. They are not just cogs in the machine. They are the foundations of a system. One that capitalises on the *netflixisation* of design, that is, the categorisation of everything through uniformisation disguised as tailored-made content. The pressure of belonging, being accepted and innovative are merged through an empire of algorithms that flatten designers' spheres of human activity into a convincingly self-indulgent, homogenous grand narrative. More than good or bad, happy or sad, this is presented as inevitable.

Design is production. It is unconceivable that to design can mean to undo, to dismantle, to destroy, to retreat. In *Conceptual Design – A Polemic* (1977), published in the context of the conference *Design for Need – The Social Contribution of Design* (1976), Brian Smith makes a case against design conferences and short-sighted good intentions: "We get into our planes and boats and trains full of enthusiasm – 'I'm going

14

to Change Design'; 'I'm going Design for peoples' Needs.' And on the way back, when boredom has set in, when the weight of papers has pressed us firmly back into our comfy chairs, we see that really we went as voyeurs. The meaning of the words changed, the cube flipped, and we listened to people talking about how design was changing, and how design is for peoples' needs, which we already knew, but fooled ourselves that we had not come to be told yet again." (Smith, 1977, p. 108) This was at a time when there weren't so many flashing screens with animations, apps, tote bags, t-shirts, banners, posters, flags, badges, pencils, pens and premium notebooks for hundreds of design events per month in several points of the globe. And here we are. Again.

Within architectural practice, there are examples in which architects chose not to design as a design act. One notorious case is that of Jean Phillipe Vassal and Anne Lacaton, who in 1996, were commissioned to renovate and embellish the Square Léon Aucoc in the city of Bordeaux, France. To the architecture duo, the square was fine as it was, surrounded with sober façades of well-designed collective public housing. Apart from minor maintenance work, nothing else was done. There was no need for up-to-date benches or lamps, or a fashionable gesture that may have been common practice at the time. In design, examples like this are rare. To the question "What should designers do?", Brian Smith answers: "apart from a few special cases, they should stop designing – at least under the present terms of reference. To the people designing doorknobs, cars, hairdriers, radios, packages, chairs, beds, and tractors and bandages, we should say 'STOP – THE ONES WE'VE GOT WILL DO'. You've been so clever, such good designers, that nearly everything we make and use is just about good enough now, considering all these other problems we've got." (Smith, 1977, p. 111) In graphic design discourse, Jeffery Keedy provocatively argues in *Hysteria*™ (2001) that "ironically, designers can make their biggest social and

15

political impact by not designing. After all, someone designs most of our ecological, social, and cultural nightmares before they are unleashed on the world." (Keedy, 2003, p. 208) In 2011, when the *Occupy Movement* started gaining international attention, a version of the logo of London's Underground was being occasionally used. Soon after people were prevented from using it, a competition to find a new one was held, with designer Jonathan Barnbrook's proposal being chosen through a public vote. Even for a progressive socio-political movement, competition and production is invariably the answer. Design, in its most immediate and *unprofessional* form, was already in use: hand-drawn basic signage, announcements and a variety of visual approaches to meet the needs of self-organisation and day-to-day activities. The movement didn't need a logo. In fact, the inexistence of one reflected its diversity, and made it difficult to be 'branded' and categorised, which contributed to its powerfulness.

The systems on which design operates are fundamentally and hypnotically flawed. They don't *just* need improvement. They don't *just* need resistance. They need complete change. Systemic change normally happens as an ultimatum, democracy in its multiple variations, protests and demonstrations, a directive from a global or continental institution. It usually takes place when there seems to be no other option. Designers, and the systems they sustain and validate, are in the business of future-making. They love to shine and also like to churn out stunningly attractive visions of the future on a daily basis, as if they were just another entry in their portfolio. The time for manifestos is out, and for *just* good intentions, too. If designers don't think about and practice design at the level of systems and put politics at the core of what they do—with climate crisis, fascism, racism, xenophobia—when we realise that we don't have any other option, there will be no future at all.

16

Introduction

In *Whatever Happened to Total Design* (1998), Mark Wigley says that total design has two meanings: first, what might be called the implosion of design, the focusing of design inward on a single intense point, converging into a structural and systematic model; second, what might be called the explosion of design, the expansion of design out to touch every possible point in the world. In both cases, there is still a desire for control, centralisation and domination.[1] Total design is a fantasy about control – of design as control – which in the turn from the first to the second half of the 20th century, in a context where systemic thinking was developing, demonstrates modern principles that set design out as driving force, guided by its formal canons, and distanced from the field of critical analysis in various aspects – cultural, political, economic or technological – and drove the practice of design itself. In *Design Systems,* Francisco Laranjo offers us an updated reading of the concept of a system, confronting the weight of its historic setting, the multiple meanings of a concept that initially suggests, in an abstract way, models of power, and then also points to a methodology of post-structural research.

The workshops led by Luiza Prado and Pedro Oliveira, Belle Phromchanya (ACED), Ruben Pater and the residency by the Demystification Committee developed approaches that characterise some of the most interesting and current critical practices in design. Installing the results of the four residencies in the public space, allowing various interactions with a broad audience is a crucial aspect – the desire to turn the proposals developed into catalysts of interpretation, questioning and discussion. It makes way for a participatory, democratic and plural dimension, based on which contemporary systems – both inside and outside design – can be questioned.

José Bártolo, Chief Curator
Porto Design Biennale 19'

1 Wigley, M. (1998) *Whatever Happened to Total Design.* In: *Harvard Design Magazine,* n.º 5 – Design, Arts and Architecture.

Design Systems
Design Research Residence Series,
Porto Design Biennale '19

The project *Design Systems,* developed in the context of the Porto Design Biennale (2019), consisted of a series of four design research residencies investigating the idea of systems in design from multiple perspectives. They aimed to offer the workshops' participants and the public, an introduction to systems thinking in design, challenging a one-dimensional view of design, stripped of its inherent relations, tensions, problems, consequences. Brazilian design researchers Luiza Prado and Pedro Oliveira held a workshop with the goal of unpacking the networks that inform the existence of an object in the world, as well as its implications in-use. This workshop was followed by a study of Portuguese news media by Thai researcher Belle Phromchanya (ACED), making use of the archives of the Municipal Library of Porto. It used cross-fields research methodologies to discover unseen patterns and collect evidence that could be constructed into a coherent narrative. Dutch designer Ruben Pater's workshop mapped, deconstructed, and visualised the means of production of contemporary graphic design in the cities of Porto and Matosinhos, and

the way economic value is created and sustained. Finally, the collective Demystification Committee, travelled to Porto to conduct field-research in the context of their project and film INTERFACE CHAOS (2019), mapping and connecting the behaviour of money through tax evasion in Porto and its infrastructure. The resulting work was installed in five metro stations in Porto during one month, between October and November 2019. The central goal of this residence series was to share with the participants different knowledge and methods, by offering exposure to multiple ways of dealing with systems thinking in design. The installations that followed partially exposed the debates and methods explored during this residency series with several participants: designers, students and educators. They also open up for debate the limitations and potential of these (design) gestures in the public space. By covering a variety of areas of interest with diverse approaches, *Design Systems* proposes an exposure to the ways in which design can analyse, deconstruct, reveal and challenge the systems in which we live and how these, in turn, design us back.

Francisco Laranjo, Curator

Workshop led by Ruben
Pater at the Shared
Institute, 2019.

Impossible Methods
Porto Metro Station: Aliados

During a 3-day workshop, we worked with participants to map networks that emerge around the making of objects, and are often obscured or suppressed. These ranged from the extraction of raw matter to the manufacturing process, culminating with the power relations and influence generated through the presence of an object in the world. In this workshop we expand the understanding of the design of an object as a delicate balance between the actors that compose this network.

As designers, we are typically trained to understand things in terms of usability, ergonomics, aesthetics, and industrial manufacturing. However, little attention is given to the political and sociocultural issues that surround an object, or that are shaped by it. These dynamics of action-reaction aren't just a matter of cause and consequence, but rather a materialisation of historical processes which, often, determine and condition the object in its current shape.

These reflections led our workshop participants to choose the low-cost airline sized suitcase as an object through which to explore issues connecting the city of Porto to the international circulation of tourists, migration routes, and Portugal's own colonial past. Together, we mapped how the presence of such an object conditions architecture, commerce, urbanism, class struggles, and gentrification in the urban space.

This installation was conceived as a composition played on the station's speakers, and a series of posters based on the maps we developed.

Luiza Prado and Pedro Oliveira

(Alojamento Local

(Alojamento Local

O PORTO NÃO SE VENDE

Installation view,
Aliados Metro Station,
Porto, October 2019.

Impartial Spectrum
Porto Metro Station: São Bento

How can a society have an informed understanding of world events? *Impartial Spectrum* is an exploration of news culture, in which notions of journalistic neutrality and the framing of global affairs are explored and challenged. This research project collects and compares different publication behaviours by international news media, situating them in the context of Portuguese news media. Four subjects were selected as case studies to be presented in this iteration: climate crisis, Hong Kong protests, anti-abortion movement, and tourism. This selection was based on the global narrative to which they are subjected to, its controversy, and because these issues have been covered in a wide range of forms, as well as a consequence of the intention to engage with both locals and visitors of Porto. The installation of 80 prints in the main hall of São Bento's metro station contains a collection of images and headlines from multiple international media sources, covering the selected cases. *Impartial Spectrum* presents diverse political and visual ways in which news are highlighted in the media, arranged by their tone of voice, ideological and political agenda, and local vs. global narrative. It aims to reveal subtle patterns and media positionings within the seemingly objective reporting, encouraging at the same time the audience to recognise the variety of ways in which news are framed in their daily news and how it influences our consumption and shapes our access to information.

ACED (Belle Phromchanya & Noortje van Eekelen)

Main lobby, São Bento
Metro Station, Porto,
October 2019.

Post Millennial Career Anxiety
Porto Metro Stations: Bolhão + Campo 24 de Agosto

So you want to become a designer? Design is a popular profession. Almost two-and-a-half thousand new students enrol in design schools in Portugal every year. The popularity of design is closely linked to romantic ideas of creativity, innovation and novelty which are nurtured in social spheres of class, family, and education. Spheres that support the needs of capitalist society for students to acquire professional skills as quickly as possible, so they can become productive citizens in the labour market.

Once you graduate, what will you do? Thousands of talented design graduates are faced with a labour market with few jobs, unpaid work, and flexible contracts. Designers are engaged in fierce competition, pressured to present themselves as productive, flexible, and as creative as possible on social media. This process of self-optimisation leads to the anxiety of not being relevant or active enough, obsessively posting and censoring work that is too personal or political in order to attract the right clients. Career anxiety runs parallel to mental health issues such as depression, which has risen in the last decades of neoliberal capitalist society.

Post Millennial Career Anxiety is a series of provocative questions and statements in the public space made during a three-day workshop in June 2019. Written and designed collectively, they critically explore the relation of design education and capitalism. By sharing them in the public space, the participants hope to engage the public by triggering and stimulating thinking about alternative models of value in design. By selecting texts which refer to general tendencies in the economy, the commercialisation of education and career anxiety, we hope they reach all those who pass by on their way to school or work.

Ruben Pater

Installation views,
Campo 24 de Agosto
and Bolhão Metro
Stations, Porto,
October 2019.

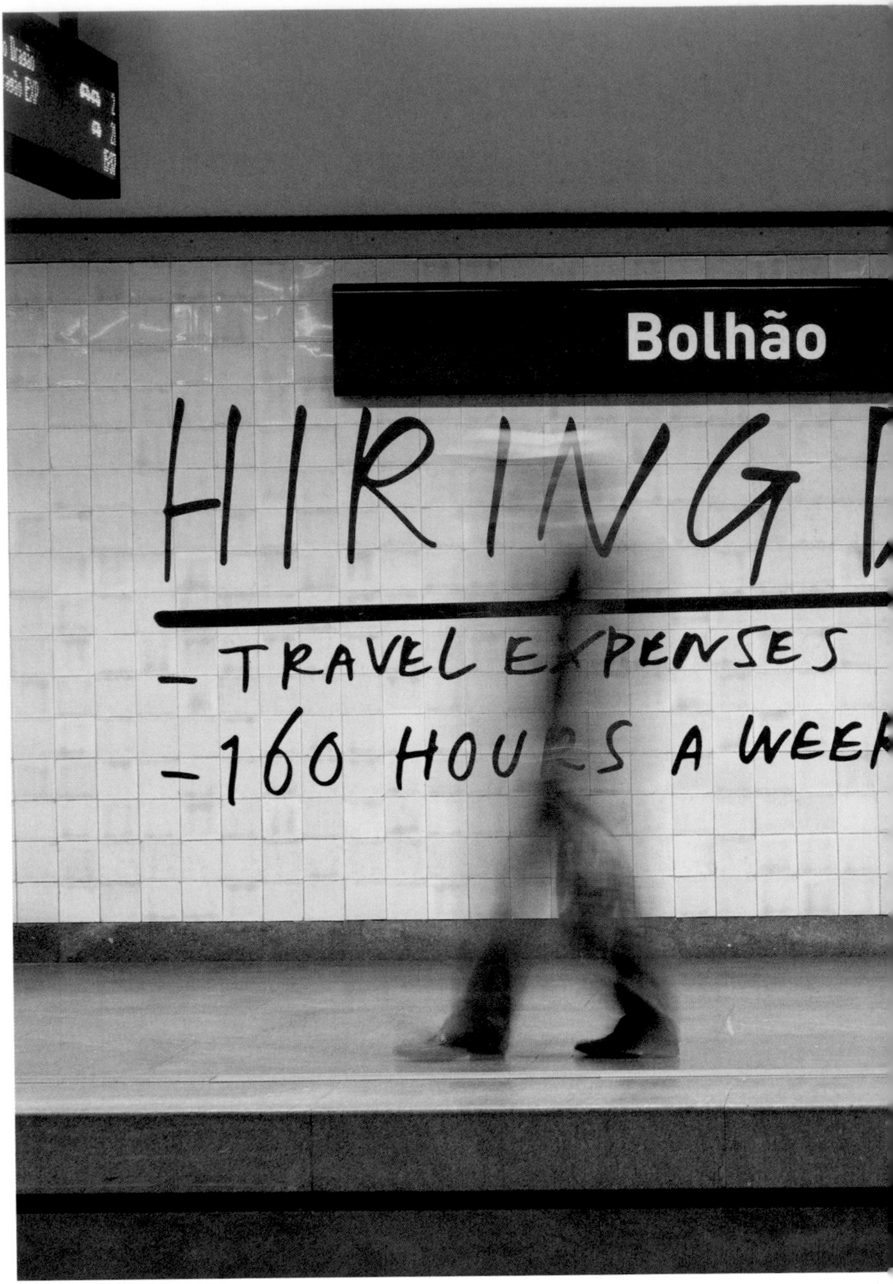
Bolhão
HIRING
_TRAVEL EXPENSES
-160 HOURS A WEEK

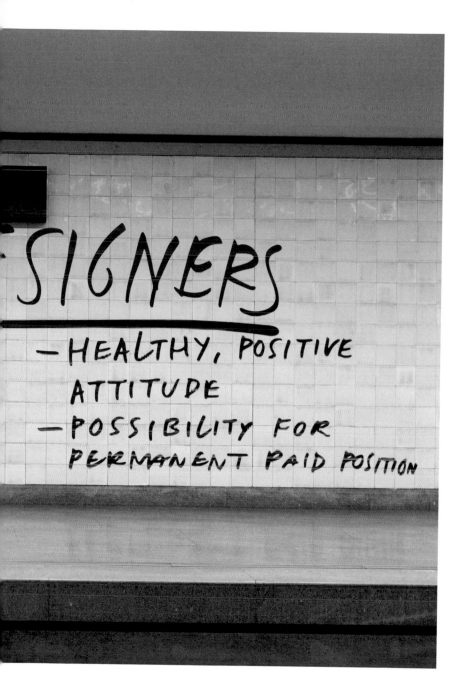

SIGNERS

- HEALTHY, POSITIVE ATTITUDE
- POSSIBILITY FOR PERMANENT PAID POSITION

31

A Chaos of Interfaces
Porto Metro Station: Trindade

Money has grown independent of its human origins. As an entity with its own intelligence and fragilities, it seeks security through a global network of 'interfaces' which enable its accumulation and exchange. Perhaps the most obvious place to find these interfaces is in tax havens, places which aid money's frictionless passage and ensure its safety.

Following a residency in summer 2019, aimed at gathering information on the local financial industry, the Demystification Committee mapped the connection between the interfaces for money's accumulation and exchange found in Porto, Portugal.

In the resulting installation, different interfaces are grouped in clusters of tiles. An interface is a local tax advisor, a shell company, an intermediary individual, or an address otherwise affiliated with a financial entity. Adjacent tiles trace the connections through which money moves or shields itself. In most cases this leaves Porto and Portugal entirely, travelling through other jurisdictions to make use of beneficial treaties and legal frameworks. There are common elements in these clusters, such as the recurring names of large accounting firms — key interfaces in the survival network of money.

A public screening of the Demystification Committee's debut short film INTERFACE CHAOS (2019) was held at the Metro Station of Campo 24 de Agosto in late October 2019. Showing money's journey for survival in another location, the tax haven of the Seychelles, the screening complemented the installation and connected these two parts of money's survival network.

Demystification Committee

Entrance hall, Trindade
Metro Station, Porto,
October 2019.

Caption on the floor:
A partial mapping of the local networks of interfaces created by money (M). Adjacent tiles mark the paths through which M moves, hides and survives: (tax) solutions, (unspecific) places, shell (companies) and (intermediary) masks.

Porto Design Biennale

Promoted by
Porto City Hall
Matosinhos City Hall
Organised by
Esad—idea, Research
in Design and Art
Board
Rui Moreira (Chairman)
Luísa Salgueiro
(Vice-Chairman)
Sérgio Afonso
Eduardo Aires
Emanuel Barbosa
Francisco Providência
José Bártolo
Maria Milano
Executive Director
Sérgio Afonso
Vice-Director
Magda Seifert
Advisory Board
Clarisse Castro
Diogo Vilar
Fernando Rocha
Guilherme Blanc
Maria José Rodrigues
Sílvia Fernandes

2019 Post Millennium Tension

Chief Curator
José Bártolo
Curatorial Assistant
Raquel Pais
Curator Territorio Italia
Maria Milano
Curatorial Assistant Territorio Italia
Eleonora Fedi
Luisa Medina
Sara Carraretto
Schools Coordinator
Francisco Providência
Satellites Coordinator
Emanuel Barbosa
Production Director
Sofia Meira
Communications Director
Mafalda Martins
Editorial Coordination
Andreia Faria
Exhibition Project Manager
Rui Canela
Graphic Design Strategy
Fábio Martins
João Castro
João Martino
Miguel Salazar
Art Director
Inês Nepomuceno
New Media Director
Diogo Vilar
Video Coordinator
André Tentúgal

Photography Coordinator
Inês d'Orey
Graphic Design
Susana Martins
Luís Cepa
New Media Design
Rafael Gonçalves
Motion Graphics
Lyft Creative Studio
Video and Photography
Tânia Franco
Fernando Miranda
Production Assistant
Íris Rebelo
Sara Pinheiro
Production Team
Alexandre Barbosa
Alexandre Costa
Carlos Rocha
Filipe Pinto
José Castro
Front Office
Margarida Antunes
Secretariat
Carla Correia
Social Media
Rita Carvalho
Press Office
This is Ground Control
Rota & Jorfida |
Communication
and PR
PDB Cafeteria
Daniela Real
PDB Stores
Coral Books

Design Systems

Curator
Francisco Laranjo
Guest Researchers
Luiza Prado
& Pedro Oliveira
Belle Phromchanya
(ACED)
Ruben Pater
Demystification
Committee
Installation Sites
Porto Metro Stations:
Aliados
São Bento
Bolhão
Campo 24 de Agosto
Trindade
Graphic Design
shared.institute
Photography
Inês d'Orey
(Photos of pages 19 and
26 by Shared Institute)

Workshop Participants
Andres Torres
Arthur Silveira Veras
Camila Monteiro
Pereira
Catarina Rodrigues
Elvia Vasconcelos
Isabela Lima
Joana Carriço
Luís Frias
Luisa Tormenta
Nuno Coelho
Rita Ribeiro
Sérgio Miguel
Magalhães
Stef Silva
Workshops' Venue
Shared Institute
Thanks
José Bártolo
Magda Seifert
Sérgio Afonso
Sofia Meira
Raquel Pais
Diogo Vilar
Inês d'Orey

One Size Fits All
Ruben Pater

A graphic designer may work like an artist, but once production gets involved, she has to assume the role of an engineer. Whatever the artistic quality or political intention of a graphic design work may be, its form will have to comply with printing specs, browsers specs, and other industry-imposed conditions. The vast majority of graphic design work has to be made reproducible for global trade and communication using standards.

The history of standardization walks parallel to the history of economy. Pre-capitalist economies made use of bespoke measurements that fit local circumstances. These were often 'human' in more than one way. The body was used as a measuring instrument (thumb, elbow, foot) and local systems had cultural and social meanings that reflected the social life of small-scale exchange. Systems that were used over centuries were considered social and even sacred. Metal or stone casts of weights and measuring units were kept secure in city halls and temples as if they were idols.

Measurement systems grew from specific local conditions. Farmers would often use different measurements depending on the soil, crop, location, sun, and slope. It made no sense to equate an acre of sandy, unfertile soil to an acre of the most productive patch of land. This is why for instance labor time was used as a land measurement, such as the French _Journal_ (a day) was the amount of land that could be plowed in a single day. (Witold, 1986) Cultures in far reaching areas like the Sahara had developed detailed measurement systems for long distances, as miscalculation would have dire consequences.

The Ashanti in Ghana developed refined measuring tools for weighing gold dust, on which their economy depended. (Ibid.)

These examples of pre-capitalist measurements systems reveal that economy is a social activity in which value is exchanged between people, creating cultural traditions and narratives in the process. Today's design systems have been both the result of industrialization and the dominance of economic efficiency, through the success of scientific and rational methods from the European Enlightenment. By virtue of such relations, power structures have emerged of Western Europe, dictating their measurements onto much of the world in the process of statecraft and capitalist trade.

This essay takes the metric system, the A-formats of paper, the shipping container, and the bar code as examples of capitalist industrial standards. By examining their histories, we can better understand the relationship between graphic design and capitalism.

One 40-millionth of the Earth

A pivotal moment in the history of standardization happened in France in 1790, when a commission was asked to come up with a system of standards for measures and weights. At the time, over seven hundred measurements were used within France, and much time and effort was spent calculating the exchange of goods. The first reason for the metric system was to simply put a more efficient national trade in place. Secondly, differences in land measurements stood in the way of a national tax code. Anthropologist James C. Scott explains in *Seeing Like a State* (1998) that local measurement practices were culturally rich and social, but not 'legible' for the state, and therefore needed to be standardized in order to be taxed.

The French nation state was a forerunner in the centralization and standardization of bureaucracy and society, as the revolutionary slogan 'one king, one law, one weight, and one measure' illustrates (Ibid.). The meter proved a monumental

38

shift, as it was decided by mathematical calculation as 1/40,000,000th of the earth's diameter. This scientific approach literally shifted the scale of trade from a regional to a planetary scale. Although the metric system was emancipatory in its ideals—it lessened the power of aristocracy—most farmers saw it as something that was conjured up by bureaucrats, who knew nothing of local contexts.

The French republic fared well with the standardization of measurements. Since the state decided how land was measured, and how crops were weighed, it could exert precise control over trade and taxes. Standardization was a way to prioritize economic efficiency over regional cultural and social relations.

Usage des Nouvelles Mesures.

1. le Litre *(Pour la Pinte)*
2. le Gramme *(Pour la Livre)*
3. le Metre *(Pour l'Aune)*
4. l'Are *(Pour la Toise)*
5. le Franc *(Pour une Livre Tournois)*
6. le Stere *(Pour la Demne Voie de Bois)*

Woodcut dated 1800 illustrating the new decimal units which became the legal norm in France on 4 November 1800, five years after the the metrical system was first introduced. In the captions, each one of these six new units is followed by the old French unit in brackets: the litre, the gram, the metre, the are (100 square metres), the franc, and the stère (1 cubic metre of wood). Credit: L. F. Labrousse (engraver), and J. P. Delion (publisher). Source: Bibliothèque nationale de France, CC license.

From Rags to Ratio

Paper sizes are very determinate for the work of graphic designers. Before the invention of the A-formats, a great number of paper formats flourished in Western Europe. Sizes were derived from the available technology and material limitations. Parchment, which was made from animal hides, was limited to the size of the skin of sheep and goats. When the first paper mills appeared in Europe, the size of the sheets depended on the reach of the arms of a worker holding the mould loaded with pulp (Kinross, 2009). Handmade paper sizes were approximate and were not known by their exact measurements. They would simply be known by names like 'Royale' or 'Imperiale', and the sizes of two sheets of 'Royale' would differ by today's standards.

It was again in France where a scientific system for paper sizes was devised in line with the metric system. It was a rational, mathematical invention based on a ratio of $1: \sqrt{2}$, as the width of two sheets would form the length of the bigger size sheet. This invention was perfected and standardized in Germany as part of the *Deutsches Institut für Normung* (German industry norms) in 1922. The DIN system was initiated in 1917 by the manufacturers for artillery to streamline the efforts to support the war industry during the First World War. Out of the many DIN industry standards still in use today, the most well-known are the paper formats which were adopted as a world standard as ISO 216 in 1975, the most used paper size system in the world; the A-formats.

In recent decades, the steady decline of printed matter has given rise to online printing services. Websites like Flyeralarm— the largest online printer in Germany—have decimated smaller print businesses. The companies' success comes from limiting choices using preselected formats; A6 for a postcard, A5 for a flyer, and A4 for folders. They have stepped into the shoes of the designer by choosing the paper size and stock for them.

Photo from the Leipzig Spring Fair 1932. At the exhibition "Office supplies and equipment" DIN presented paper sizes as a system-building standard under the heading "Normformate helfen verkaufen", (standard sizes increase sales). The idea was to encourage manufacturers to use standard formats in manufacturing to increase sales. Source: National Library of Sweden, CC Llicense.

Standardization by online printers has led to downward-spiralling prices for printed material, which makes it almost impossible for graphic designers to argue for quality print work in custom sizes at local print shops. If a client is not flush with money, a designer may find herself limited to the formats that cheap bulk printers offer. Secondly, the low cost makes large print runs more attractive than small print runs, leading to outsourcing and more paper waste. Printed matter is used as a cheap standardized surface to steamroll other forms of communication by its sheer volume.

The War Box

Another revolution in standardization that accelerated global capitalist trade was the shipping container. Through its ubiquity, it has become a symbol of world trade and efficient transportation of cheap goods — well before it became the standard for temporary hipster locations like pop-up coffee

41

bars and festivals. Ninety percent of the world trade is now handled through shipping, and the low price of the transport of goods can be attributed — together with the cheap extraction of resources — to the invention of the shipping container. Even the volume of shipping trade itself is measured in TEU (twenty-foot equivalent), the cargo capacity of a 20-foot-long container.

Ports looked very different before the container industry. Large crews of longshoremen were needed to pack cargoes into ships, workers that lived close to the harbor. The implementation of the container in the 1960s made the large shipyard crews obsolete, turning harbors into parking lots for cranes and trucks. In the fifteen years after the shipping container was implemented, 90% of dockworkers in New York were laid off.

The container had been in use since the 1900s on trains and boats for coal transport. It was the Vietnam war (1955–1975) that sped up its global distribution (Hardt & Negri, 2017). At the height of the war, more than half a million US troops were deployed in Vietnam, which required a massive logistics operation. South Vietnam did not have an international shipping infrastructure at the time, and the US military had difficulty supplying its troops. They hired Sealand—the first container shipping line—to take care of the transport using square containers nicknamed CONEX boxes.

Container shipping for the US military accounted for half of the company's turnover in 1970. Pacific shipping routes carrying weapons and military material for the Vietnam war laid the groundwork for the trade of goods between Asia and the US. Sealand itself was sold to Maersk in 1999 to form the world's largest container shipping company.

Sea freight has strict guidelines for packaging, wrapping, bulk weights and sizes. The measurements of containers dictate the shape of boxes and packages, and the use of materials to make products suitable for long sea journeys.

The low cost of shipping has outsourced a large part of the printing industry to low-wage countries, making printing thousands of miles away cheaper than printing locally.

Use of the FB-CC01 Container Express (CONEX) Container, nicknamed CONEX box. It was developed by the U.S. Army in late 1952. By 1965, the US military had some 100,000 CONEX boxes, and by 1967, over 100,000 more were used in Vietnam. Source: Vietnam Studies, Logistic Support by Lieutenant General Joseph M. Heiser, Jr. Department of the Army, Washington DC, US, 1991.

The Black and White Stripes

In packaging design the bar code has been a very influential standard. Now found on every imaginable product, the bar code was an invention of engineer Joe Woodland when he was a graduate student in 1952. Woodland was inspired by Morse code, and once, as he was sitting on Miami Beach, he drew his fingers in the sand and came up with the idea that the strips could be thick or thin (Weightman, 2015). Bar codes uses optical scanning, measuring the different white spaces which correspond to a unique product.

It wasn't until the mid-1970s in the midst of the oil crisis, labour unrest, and recession, that the bar code was implemented on a mass scale (Parenti, 2003). The biggest US supermarket chains held a meeting to standardize product codes. The bar code was selected out of several proposals to reverse the plummeting sales. Despite initial costs of installing bar code scanners, the profits soon outweighed the costs. The return on investment turned out to be a staggering 41,5%.

While economic efficiency is undoubtedly the main achievement of the bar code, the collection of consumer data is its most important legacy. Real-time sales information meant faster logistics and better insights in customer behaviour. Advertising and product development could respond to consumer demand almost immediately, with a minimum of under- or overstocking. In terms of engineering, the bar code has successfully devised a visual system that can be applied everywhere in the world independently of social contexts.

Through its ability to track consumer data, the bar code has entered all areas of life, even newborn babies are scanned at hospitals using bar codes. You can put a bar code on anything and it can be tracked, traced, and valued using computation and algorithmic efficiency. This is how the bar code has succeeded in becoming the logo of international trade.

Against Standardized Living
If we look at the history of the metric system, the A-format paper sizes, the container, and the barcode, we find that these forms of standardization are also forms of simplification, where information about the social context of work and production is lost in the process. As each item in industrial production needs to be identical to all the others, traces of labor and human interaction are made invisible, which prevents those working to assemble or produce the object any emotional or personal connection.

The measurement systems that were used before the metric system reveal that pre-capitalist knowledge held tremendous value and knowledge about local contexts. Informal knowledge is still produced every day, but usually not recognized as legitimate. Communication is always social and in flux. Allowing more informal forms of knowledge to be used in graphic design can challenge the industrial monopoly on communication and focus more on its social function than merely be a vehicle to create profit.

With paper, we see that graphic design is a creative profession that is limited by the standards that the industry has set. Choices in colours, sizes, materials, and shapes are provided by manufacturers of industrial production, whether physical or digital. By using Flyeralarm formats instead of working with a local printer to create a custom design, the designer accepts a lower quality and diminishes social relations. Printers close, graphic services are outsourced and monopolized. A socially aware graphic design should be able to look beyond industrial pre-sets.

The quest for lower production costs and profits has driven innovations like the container and the barcode. Just two examples in a range of technologies which are devised to streamline logistics for optimal economic efficiency. Efficiency which is based on cheap fossil fuels, because what is efficient about a book being designed in Europe, printed in China, and sold in North America? Expansion and outsourcing can only exist because of standardization. If wages become too high in South East Asia, production can be moved immediately to East Africa with little change to the entire operation. If we seriously want to address graphic design's involvement in creating waste and inequality, then perhaps mass-production should not be its primary goal. Questioning standardization should be a part of that.

Beyond doubt, industrial innovation is necessary, convenient, and makes a lot of processes easier, especially when working with large groups of people. It is not really useful nor better to create a new paper format or a new typographic measurement for each new design, or to use a different paper size for everything. But we should remember that global industry standards have allowed for global mass production cycles and outsourcing to take place. This has created a lot of wealth but also alienated workflow, promoted exploitation of labor and a climate crisis that demands us to produce less, more local, and in a more socially meaningful manner.

The possibility of design systems that question its capitalist foundations, start with the realization that economy is essentially a social activity in which value is exchanged between people. A move towards a non-capitalist practice of design will therefore have to question the very basics of how design is practiced without necessarily going back to pre-industrial production. Other forms of knowledge-production can emerge from questioning standards and measurements, from the search for alternative ways of working that strengthen social bonds and relations, not break them.

This essay is a pre-publication of the book *CAPS LOCK: Graphic Design Under Capitalism* by Ruben Pater, which is scheduled for publishing in 2020 by Valiz, Amsterdam, NL.

Bibliography

· Anderson, B. (1983) *Imagined Communities*, London: Verso Books.
· Drucker, J. & McVarish, E. (2009) *Graphic Design History: A Critical Guide*, Pearson.
· Hardt, M. & Negri, A. (2017) *Assembly*, Oxford: Oxford University Press.
· Kinross, R. (2009) *A4 and Before Towards a Long History of Paper Sizes*, NIAS.
· Kula, W. (1986) *Measures and Men*, Princeton University Press.
· Lee, C. (2017) *This Was Written On Stolen Indigenous Land*. In: Decolonising Design (web). Available at: https://www.decolonisingdesign. com/guest-contributions/2017/ guest-post-this-was-written-on- stolen-indigenous-land/
· Madrigal, A (2017) *Episode 1: Welcome to Global Capitalism*, In: Medium (web). Available at: https:// medium.com/containers/episode- 1-welcome-to-global-capitalism- f9f56c92f414
· Parenti, C. (2003) *The Soft Cage: Surveillance in American from Slavery to the War on Terror*. New York: Basic Books.

· Print Business, Eds. (2017) The runners and riders in online printing. In: Print Business (web). Available at: https://printbusiness.co.uk/news/ The-runners and riders in-online- printing/107954
· Scott, J. (1998) *Seeing Like a State*, Yale University Press.
· *The British Newspaper Archive*. Available at: https://www. britishnewspaperarchive.co.uk/ titles/poor-mans-guardian.
· Weightman, G. (2019) *The History of the Bar Code*. In: *Smithsonian Magazine*. Available at: https://www. smithsonianmag.com/innovation/ history-bar-code-180956704

Fluttering Code: A Cultural and Aesthetic History of the Split-flap Display
Shannon Mattern

There's something cinematic about the split-flap display, with its thousands of tiny panels – each featuring a painted or silkscreened character – fluttering around a central drum. You can imagine one flickering in the background of an airport scene, in a film set in the heyday of air travel, its rotating letters and numbers spelling out a grammar of geographic possibility: Addis Ababa, Gate 6; Lima, Gate 17. We Americans of a certain age and location remember their anticipatory shiver on the transit boards in Amtrak's Northeast Corridor stations. The displays' small, moving, analog parts sounded out and performed time's sifting and fluttering passage; their choreography triggered and metered the frantic ballet of harried commuters rushing about below. As reporter Sarah Laskow (2016) notes, split-flap boards "evoke a sense of anticipation …[and] reassurance – soon, that train or plane will take you away, and you'll be going somewhere."

Over the last two decades, most public split-flaps have been replaced by glowing LCD screens, many of them installed by the same company, Solari, that pioneered the old-school mechanism in the 1950s, then adapted it for the digital age. Yet several electromechanical installations continue to chug along in the train stations and airports of Europe and Asia. And a few new boards have appeared – bespoke displays created for restaurants and museums, for the offices of nostalgic tech companies and the homes of wealthy private collectors. New split-flap start-ups have appeared, too: Vestaboard exhibits information from your Twitter, Slack, or Google Calendar accounts; configures its flaps into multihued geometric patterns; and responds to verbal commands from a voice assistant. This next-generation split-flap networks our personal devices and personal data to public displays. Several artists have adopted the split-flap, too, exploring the materiality of code, and its capacity to produce productive and pleasurable inefficiencies, in an age of flat screens and algorithmic immediacy. Across these applications, historical and contemporary, we see that the split-flap constitutes an adaptable design system – one that extends long traditions of public reading, while also broadcasting messages and embodying operational logics germane to the computational age.

Electromechanical Echoes
In 1903, when many railway stations used chalkboards and bulletin boards – and even "men or phonographs" – to call out arrivals and departures, New Yorker Eugene Fitch patented a cylindrical glass clock, lantern-like in form, that featured "indicating-plates... pivotally mounted upon a rotating part." (Blake & Jackson, 1917; Fitch, 1903; Mackey, n.d.) His Plato clock – named after its metal plates, not the philosopher – inspired a host of consumer flip-clock designs throughout the 20th century. Meanwhile, Solari, the "Old and Awarded Tower Clock Company," had been making, well, tower clocks amidst the dolomite mountains in Pesariis, Italy, since 1725. These large public audiovisual interfaces served to orient and synchronize entire neighborhoods and towns. In 1948, two of the six Solari brothers, Fermo and Remigio, built a new factory in Udine, where Remigio began experimenting with the flap unit. Over the next decades, Solari Udine, in collaboration with designers Gino Valle, Michele Provinciali, and Massimo Vignelli, produced its own selection of award-winning table-top flip clocks: the Cifra, Emera, and Dator, all of which became coveted collectors' items.[1] (Delavan, 2016; "History," n.d.; "Manuals," n.d.; "Time Keeper," n.d.) The Cifra 3 was acquired by the Museum of Modern Art and, in 2015, put back into production.

As Solari's first clock, the Cifra 5, appeared in 1956, the company was also implementing the split-flap on a much larger scale – which seems fitting, given their familiarity with grand public timepieces. Amelio Candussio, a Solari Product Specialist stationed in Long Island City, New York, told us that the company fielded a request from a Belgian train system to install a transit information display system – featuring destinations, tracks, and times – in the Liège-Guillemins Railway Station. (Candussio, 2019) And that's where the public flip-board began its multi-decade journey, ultimately appearing in countless railway stations and airports around the globe and compelling new modes of "public reading." (Fritzsche, 2009; Henkin, 1998). Along the way, Solari was joined by a few competitors: Conrac, Omega, Bodet, and Pragotron. (Bodet, 1974; Lagasse and Geissler, 1973)

The split-flap's spread coincided with the so-called "golden age" of commercial air travel, and Solari boards hung in two of its temples: Eero Saarinen's TWA terminal at JFK Airport in New York, and his Dulles International Airport in Washington, D.C. Another boon was the 1971 emergence of Amtrak, which sought to revive American rail travel and refresh stations long neglected by their former private owners. "There had been so little investment that many stations still relied on chalkboards to list their arrivals and departures," design critic Inga Saffron reports. Amtrak – and other national and regional rail systems – often replaced their existing signage with "modern and mod" Solari boards, which "changed the way time is presented." (Saffron, 2018) Thus, while more and more passengers were crossing continents and circumnavigating the globe at record speeds, a geophysical rendering of time – via the traditional round clock face – made way for flickering lines of code. Code and encryption were crucial to the Cold War context from which the split-flap arose – and data processing was becoming ever more central to the expanding realm of global logistics.

TWA Terminal at JFK Airport, New York, US, 1962.
©Solari di Udine Spa

Candussio told us that Solari's boards also lived – or, in some cases, *still* live – in the Barcelona stock exchange, at a Macau ferry terminal, in a courthouse in Naples, at the dog races in Hong Kong, at a university basketball arena, and in movie theaters throughout Italy and South Africa.[2] In each case, the audio-visual flutter signaled an urgent information update: a new stock price, a new score, a new case in the courtroom down the hall. In 1973, Solari made three huge boards for the Philadelphia convention center, but then couldn't fit them through the doors. Candussio isn't sure what happened to them. Split-flap displays from a variety of makers also appeared on election night news specials, and on 1970s and 80s game shows like *Family Feud*.

Today, a few stations and terminals still house functional installations. Secaucus, New Jersey, maintains a collection of boards, each a different color, corresponding to the various lines of the New Jersey Transit system. (Candussio, 2019)

The Trenton and Atlantic City rail stations – and the Jacksonville, FL, airport – have working Solari boards, too. Yet maintenance of the old electromechanical devices has proven a challenge. As the company explains, a flap unit "consists of a stepper motor, which drives a flap drum and a control system with integrated electronic sensors," all of which is handled by a main controller. (Solari Udine) Each part represents a vulnerability. "Even if we normally maintain these kinds of boards for 20 or 30 years," Candussio told us, "there are some cases where some components are no [longer] available."

That hasn't stopped the station managers in Łódź, Poland, which has built up a local economy to keep its split-flap display spinning. The system runs on punch cards made by a local printer, and the punching pliers, which are in heavy use, require replacement pins made by a local locksmith. Parts of the card reader wear out regularly, too, and the assembly requires regular dusting. "It's an electromechanical signaling system managed and updated by human operators," Donald Papp (2016) writes (see also Tyszecki, 2016).

LCD Logistics

Rather than kludging together salvaged parts to maintain a functional system, most stations opt instead for an upgrade to newer display technologies. Solari adapted its split-flap for LED/LCD and electromagnetic "flip-dot" displays. The old electromechanical sign in Philadelphia's Penn Station, Amtrak's last survivor, was "controlled by computers running Windows 95 and has been known to fail for months at a time." ("30th Street Station," 2019; Rinde, 2018) The new board, installed in January 2019, promises to facilitate future tech upgrades, comply with the Americans with Disabilities Act, and modernize the station. While the old split-flap now resides at the Railroad Museum of Pennsylvania in Lancaster County, the new board streams listings across a triptych of conjoined LCD screens. The seams between those screens introduce small misalignments in the text (which, again, seems fitting, given the errancy of American train travel), but there's also a space at the bottom of the board that allows for live transcription of announcements read over the public-address system. Typographic glitches seem a small price to pay for increased accessibility.

New Haven replaced its split-flap in 2014. And New York's Penn Station, which had installed a digital homage to the split-flap in the early 2000s, abandoned the analog pretense and adopted a constellation of glaring LCDs in 2016. (Blakemore, 2016) As Amtrak (2017) explained, the new Passenger Information Display System (PIDS) consists of two large screens installed at both ends of the concourse, and 38 additional monitors distributed throughout the station, which serve to "draw traffic away from the center of the room." While such a topology promises decreased congestion and smoother passenger flows, it also sacrifices a communal focal point and a synchronizing rhythm — what Saffron calls a "spinning, clacking, pre-digital hearth." We used to meet traveling companions "under the board."

And, as Saffron (2018) recalls, we also waited for the "satisfying clickety-clack of the flaps, which echo the clickety-clack of the trains as they race along the tracks. The mechanical board [was] the physical manifestation of motion." Now, the LCDs' digital motion — the screen refresh, the chromatic flip of a pixel — is too fast for the human eye to discern. There's no cue or "push notification" for the arrival of a new datum: a newly assigned track number or updated departure time. And without that audio-visual flutter, that call to attention, we don't know when to look up — so we stare at the screen, waiting for something to happen, just as we stare at the hundreds of other glowing rectangles that populate our public and private environments.[3]

This electromechanical-to-digital transition extends beyond the "big boards" in urban central stations. Solari has also provided all the digital countdown clocks throughout the

New York City subways; the kiosks at Metro North stations; and all of the Long Island Railroad's digital transit signage in Penn Station, Jamaica Station in Queens, and Atlantic Terminal in Brooklyn. These new signs are typically bright and clean and flat and silent, their high-resolution graphics suggesting a degree of accuracy and efficiency that rickety 20th-century transit infrastructure can't always deliver. Thus, we still perch at the edge of the platform, peering down the tunnel, waiting for a glimpse of oncoming headlights – a old-school analog signaling system.

Commuters longing for the boards' haptic flutter can visit a website that allows them to recreate the sights and sounds of a split-flap sign displaying real-time information from any Amtrak station.[4] Solari found that several clients sought to integrate similarly nostalgic simulation in their replacement displays. Newark's board – a video wall composed of 16 monitors – is a digital split-flap replica, complete with clickety-clacking sound effects. Boston's digital sign, installed in 2004, emits a sonic flutter, too. These skeuomorphic displays, which digitally reference their analog precedents, allow for both the promised efficiencies and precision of 21st-century data management, while also gesturing toward the haptic engagement and charisma of the beloved 20th-century interface.

Mechanical Flaps in an Algorithmic Age

Solari is still making split-flaps, Candussio told us – but only for "special cases," for which they offer "complete customization." Clients can choose small, medium, or large mechanisms with 40, 60, or 80 flaps in plastic or aluminum, printed in an array of typefaces, and arranged in varying numbers of rows and columns. As developer Tyler Morse was transforming Saarinen's 1962 TWA Terminal into the TWA Hotel, he turned to Solari to create two new split-flap displays for the lobby and lounge. The hotel opened in 2019, inciting quite a nostalgic flutter. Solari has also created boards for the

San Francisco Ferry Building, and for Starbucks in Milan: 13 lines and 64 columns of letters in a custom green, spelling out menu items and special promotions. ("Starbucks Open," 2018) Custom split-flaps also appear in the National World War II Museum in New Orleans, in breweries and restaurants, at the Winter 2018-19 Fendi runway show at Milan Fashion Week, and at the Literaturmuseum in Marbach am Necker, Germany, where the board, designed in collaboration with writer Hans Magnus Enzensberger, serves as a "poesieautomat" – an automatic poetry generator. (de Vries, 2010) Split-flap start-up Oat Foundry, meanwhile, created a custom board for the Grow with Google digital skills training center in New York, where the display serves pedagogical and marketing purposes – it renders digital technologies mechanically comprehensible and cultivates a relatable physical character for the brand – while it also, according to its creators, "adds an element of magic to information."

Information's magic – or its opposite: demystification. These are among the concerns of contemporary artists deploying split-flap technology to comment on digital culture, global transit, and public communication. (Laskow, 2016) In its early days, the split-flap embodied the operative logics of an emerging computational era, the rhetorics of Cold War code, and the mechanics and affect of new means of global travel. Today, as many artists demonstrate, that same split-flap technology reminds us of digital technology's materiality – its composition of bits and packets, the electronic routes and physical geographies those units traverse, and the various temporalities inherent in computation.

In order to understand how these repurposed displays function, we can draw from decades of criticism and scholarship on digital textuality, electronic literature, installation art, and public screens; this work urges us to attend to the installations' materiality, operational logics, sensorial registers, and physical contexts, while also examining the flaps' textual content through close reading and critical interpretation. The work of N. Katherine Hayles (2008), Rita Raley (2009a, 2009b), Roberto Simanowski (2011), and others, also reminds us that most split-flap artists are engaging with critical concepts and aesthetic conceits common within digital art and poetics – yet the specificity of the medium, the fluttering display, here adds a distinctive spin.

Some split-flap artworks aim simply to display digital content in new contexts.[5] At the 2019 South by Southwest festival, artist Naho Matsuda installed *EVERY THING EVERY TIME,* a split-flap display that drew from roughly 200 data feeds: festival schedules, logistical information for nearby businesses, local weather, public service notices, global commodity prices, President Trump's Twitter feed, random statistics, and a variety of other sources. As Chris Ip (2019) proposes in *Engadget,* Matsuda's "algorithmic poetry" represents everything the "smart city could potentially see" – from civic message boards to official alert systems to Internet-of-Things-linked devices. Such a volume of information isn't humanly processable, yet Matsuda makes it material, empirical, and legible by sampling from the data-stream, revealing individual characters at an "annoyingly slow" pace, and then erasing each poem seconds after it was complete. "The ephemerality focuses your attention on it," Ip says.

EVERY THING EVERY TIME (2018),
Naho Matsuda.
R&D in collaboration with Raskl.
Photos: Jack Storey

LAb(au)'s *Signal to Noise* (2010) also engages with fleetingness and algorithmic meaning-making. The artists created a cyclorama-like installation consisting of four rows of stripped-down flap modules salvaged from a Belgian train station. As those modules spin at variable speeds through random characters, the sheer volume of mechanical operations and computational processing is rendered palpably audible. When an algorithm detects that an English word of three or more letters has appeared on adjacent modules – a signal amidst all the noise – those flaps hold their position for a few beats. (Frank, 2013; LAb[au] (n.d.)) The piece implicitly questions the logics and methods of massive data collection, and it highlights the labor and energy required for its processing. *Signal to Noise's* limited reading public – a self-selecting group in a gallery – reads signals on two levels: in waiting to crack the occasional intelligible code, visitors hear and feel the electrical signals that generate it.

Marco de Mutiis further atomizes bits of information in his *Arrivals* (2012-13), a site-specific installation hosted at Videotage, a new media art center near the old Kai Tak airport site in Hong Kong. In piecing together archival records and locals' memories of the old Hong Kong International Airport, de Mutiis realized that he had created a "database of fragments," demonstrating that "meaning … is unavoidably lost in time, unreachable, corrupted by our imperfect memories." To manifest that incomplete history, he acquired the old Solari board from the Verona train station, had it shipped to Hong Kong, broke it apart into its individual flap modules, and distributed those modules throughout the Videotage space. Dangling from the ceiling and crawling across the walls, the modules were tied together via messy tangles of bright red wire. *Arrivals* embodies the distribution and convergence of material networks, as well as the dissolution and collaging of memories. And the clacking of its split-flaps seems to function as a foreboding metronome, counting down the potential (or eventual) erasure of our recollections and repositories.[6] (de Mutiis, n.d.1; n.d.2)

A variety of other split-flap projects explore themes of movement and migration. Atlanta's Lucky Penny dance company commissioned a custom split-flap board for their "Dearly Departures" performance (2014), in which dancers occasionally mimic the machine's movements, reminding us of how sensing machines continually surveil and dissect our movements, and they highlight those aspects of our organic physiology that defy computational modeling.[7] George Sánchez-Calderón's *The Family of Man* (2010) deploys Boston's old Solari board. Its wall of flaps flip in militaristic synchrony through an array of possible destinations, ultimately settling on "Providence": all trains lead to God, yet all, paradoxically, depart at 6:66 – an impossibly fraught time. The board then offers a lineup of our contemporary deities: a list of 43 financial institutions. Shilpa Gupta's *24:00:01* (2010-12) uses a modest, single-row split-flap to unfurl a narrative about travel and belonging, security and national identity. Writing in the first-person singular – "I look out and wait for the train to go by" – while incorporating misspellings, omissions, and irregular spacing, Gupta transforms a medium typically used to broadcast objective logistical information into a poignant personal travel diary. *24:00:01* makes personal time public – like a personal split-flap alarm clock scaled up to a clocktower.

Other installations exploit the pacing and publicness of the board to facilitate communal composition and collective storytelling.[8] Artist Janet Zweig collaborated with over 100 Milwaukeeans to create short, quotidian films – workers climbing ladders and descending into manholes, neighbors shoveling show – which were then adapted for a split-flap-based public art installation. The artist created five kiosks that were affixed to lamp posts downtown; those kiosks contained several viewing windows, each hosting a Solari mechanism that offered an intimate view of a flip-book animation. *Pedestrian Dramas* (2011) scaled-down the public display technology for semi-private consumption in public places. (Carter, 2011; Schumacher, 2009) It also offered a media-history lesson, evoking the material and mechanical foundations of animation, moving pictures, and digital media forms.[9]

Finally, some split-flap artists eschew narrative and semantics – they reject the tools' historical purpose of conveying timely information – and instead use the mechanism to center the act of perception, or to perform the passage of time. For *Automated Colour Field* (2011), Rebecca Baumann took 100 flip-clocks and replaced their numbered flaps with colored cards, which arrange themselves into new chromatic configurations every minute. Similarly, Peter Wegner's split-flap installation *Monument to Change as It Changes* (2011) is composed, according to the artist, of "steel, polycarbonate, and time." It consists of 2,048 colored flaps that, every eight hours, flip through an array of unique chromatic patterns. Just as Mutiis deployed split-flap boards as mnemonic or archival devices, and as the 18th-century Solari timepieces served as local landmarks, Wegner uses his board as a monument: "Usually, monuments commemorate past events... But what if a monument instead commemorated the process of change?" ("Monument to Change," 2011; Wegner, 2011)

Perhaps this is precisely what the split-flap display was always meant to be: an embodiment of, a monument to, continual change. Yet its change isn't one of seamless digital transition – the gradual fades and automatic updates we see on today's LCD screens. The split-flap wears out; its mechanisms atrophy and require maintenance or replacement. The software and data sets feeding it content need repair and cleaning. Those artists who've chosen the split-flap as their medium often evoke this glitchy fragility – and they remind us that such precarity isn't unique to outmoded 20th-century electromechanical technologies. It's endemic to today's digital tools, too. Our liquid displays and artificially intelligent agents and connected devices are also building on assemblages of fragile material technologies.

What's more, these split-flap artists reinterpret mobility for a digital age. Whereas early transit boards, through their form and content, signaled movement and symbolized the possibilities of global travel, many of today's modified displays reference the movement of pixels and the mechanical filtering of data. Their clicketyclack, which once echoed trains coming down the track, today underscores the sounds of planetary computation: those endless rows of whirring servers that make it possible for us to book a plane ticket, send an email, or feed real-time data to a Solari board reborn.

The mechanical multisensoriality of the Solari split-flap also signals the persistence of a particular kind of haptic public reading that we find evidenced in ancient public oratory and architectural inscriptions, in the new mass publications hawked on street corners and posted on public kiosks in the 19th century, and in the open-air book markets of many contemporary cities. (See Mattern, 2017) Public literacy has long been dynamic and embodied. It has oriented the public's gaze, directed its movement, underscored its rhythms. Solari, as its name implies, illuminates the importance of these public texts.

Acknowledgements

Thank you to my research assistant Erin Simmons for her invaluable contributions. I'm also indebted to Peter Oleksik, Associate Media Conservator at the Museum of Modern Art, Caroline Gil, fellow in media conservation at MoMA, and Amelio Candussio and Elisa Zamarian at Solari, for being so generous with their time and expertise. The following Twitter colleagues also recommended helpful resources: Julian Hanna (@julianisland); Ilinca Laruscu (@ilincalaruscu); Dorrian Porter (@dgp); Jessica Priemus (@jessicapriemus).

1 The Cifra 5 clock, designed by Gino Valle, won the Compasso d'Oro award at the Milan International Furniture Fair, and the Cifra 3, which Valle designed in 1965, was acquired by the Museum of Modern Art."

2 The company also created a display for a "very rich man" in upstate New York, who has used the board to announce guests as they arrive at his social events; Candussio and his colleagues recently visited to make some repairs.

3 As technologists Adrian McEwen and Hakim Cassimally (2013) explain in their guide to *Designing the Internet of Things*, technologies' "noisy 'side effects' are something that we should ... be way of losing with a move to 'better technology.'" Without the clacking of a split-flap, "passengers waiting in a station terminal must stare endlessly up at the display, waiting for their train to be announced, rather than attending to other tasks and checking the departure board only when a change occurs."

4 Amtrak Station Status Boards: http://dixielandsoftware.net/Amtrak/solari/.

5 Artist duo Thomson & Craighead experimented with similar applications over a decade ago: *BEACON* displayed live web searches from around the world on three platforms: a website, automatedbeacon.net, born in 2005; a live data projection, launched in 2006; and a split-flap display, installed at the British Film Institute in 2007. Solari created the display, which streamed searches at a much slower pace than on the other platforms – one per minute – thus perhaps encouraging a close reading of these strings of terms, which ultimately constitute a diagnostic language: studying others' searches allows us to reflect on our collective information-seeking logics and interests, our desires and fears. (see Cohen, 2017; Moss, 2008).

6 Like de Mutiis's *Arrrivals*, Cheryl Sim's *YMX: Migration, Land, and Loss after Mirabel* (2017) eulogizes a lost airport, the Montréal-Mirabel International Airport, and recounts tales of displacement and forced migration that took place there. The installation's two bright yellow Solari displays, which once lived at YMX, "mutter to one another about land, policy, resistance, home, flight, and politics." (See Evering, 2017; "Solari Schematics," 2017). Concordia University's Matt Soar, director of the Montréal Signs Project, collects Solari boards and procured those used in Sim's exhibition. terms, which ultimately constitute a diagnostic language: studying others' searches allows us to reflect on our collective information-seeking logics and interests, our desires and fears. (see Cohen, 2017; Moss, 2008).

7 See Daniel Rozin's Interactive Art -- http://www.smoothware.com/danny/ and Hsin Chien Huang's *The Moment We Meet* (2013), which aims to use close-up portraits, rendered on a split-flap display, to demonstrate the spread of emotion and connection among our acquaintances and loved ones, and also perhaps inadvertently hints at the operationalization of facial physiognomy in 19th-century phrenology and today's facial recognition technologies. (See Huang, n.d.)

8 See *The Madeira Story Generator*, which used a Solari board at the local airport as "a medium for supporting Exquisite Corpse" – a compositional method wherein contributors add to the collective project in sequence, by looking only at what their immediate predecessors contributed. The project was designed to "revive storytelling practices within public space," which its organizers regard as an integral part of Madeiran culture. (Jorge et. al., 2003; "MStoryG," n.d.).

9 Similarly, Mark Rosen and Wendy Marvel's and Juan Fontanive's kinetic flip books remind us of the zoetrope, Eadweard Muybridge's motion studies, and other precursors to animation and automation.

Bibliography

· 6ABC Action News (2019) *30th Street Station's Split-Flap Board Finds New Home at Railroad Museum*. Available at: https://6abc.com/society/30th-street-stations-split-flap-board-finds-new-home/5429566/

· Amtrak (2017) *New Displays to Be Installed at Penn Station*. [blog] Available at: http://blog.amtrak.com/2017/01/penn-station-train-status-displays-receive-a-makeover/

· Baumann, R. (2011) *Automated Colour Field*. Museum of Contemporary Art Australia. Available at: https://www.mca.com.au/artists-works/works/2011.20/

· Blake, H. W. & Jackson, W. (1917) *Electric Railway Transportation*, 1st ed. McGraw-Hill.

· Blakemore, E. (2016) *Now Departing: Some of America's Most Iconic Train Signs*. Smithsonian. Available at: https://www.smithsonianmag.com/smart-news/now-departing-some-americas-most-iconic-train-signs-180960294/

· Bodet, P. (1974) *Timepiece with Automatic Calendar*. United States Patent and Trademark Office US 3834151. Available at: https://patents.google.com/patent/US3834151

· Candussio, A. (2019) *Interview*, October 8, 2019.

· Carter, C. (2011) *Janet Zweig's 'Pedestrian Dramas'*. In: *Shepherd Express*. Available at: https://shepherdexpress.com/arts-and-entertainment/visual-art/janet-zweig-s-pedestrian-drama/

· Chester E.; Lagasse and Francis X, Geissler. (1973) *Split Flap Display Module*. United States Patent and Trademark Office, US 3771242. Available at: https://patents.google.com/patent/US3771242A/en

· Cohen, K. (2017) *Never Alone, Except for Now: Art, Networks, Populations*. Duke University Press.

· Delavan, T. (2016) *The Clock That Time Cannot Improve*. In: *New York Times Style Magazine*. Available at: https://www.nytimes.com/2016/09/06/t-magazine/design/cifra-3-clock.html?partner=bloomberg

· de Mutiis, M. (n.d) *Arrivals*. Available at: https://demutiismarco.tumblr.com/arrivals;

· de Mutiis, M. *Arrivals*, archive. Available at: https://demutiismarco.tumblr.com/flaps.

· de Vries, E. (2010) *Poesieautomat*. YouTube. Available: https://www.youtube.com/watch?v=k0ovJAopgGU

· Evering, D. (2017) *YMX: Migration, Land, and Loss After Mirabel – Cheryl Sim*. Available at: http://danicaevering.com/YMX-Migration-Land-and-Loss-after-Mirabel-Cheryl-Sim-2017

· Fitch, E. (1903) *Clock*. United States Patent and Trademark Office, US 724460A. Available at: https://patents.google.com/patent/US724460

· Frank, A. (2013) *The Infinite Monkey Theorem Comes to Life*. In: *NPR Cosmos & Culture*. Available at: https://www.npr.org/sections/13.7/2013/12/10/249726951/the-infinite-monkey-theorem-comes-to-life

· Fritzsche, P. (2009) *Reading Berlin 1900*. Harvard University Press.
Henkin, D. (1998) *City Reading: Written Words and Public Spaces in Antebellum New York*. Columbia University Press.
· Gupta, S. (2010–12) *24:00:01*. Available at: https://shilpagupta.com/240001-2/
· Hsin-Chien, H (2013) *The Moment We Meet*. Available at: https://www.storynest.com/pix/_4proj/i_meet/p0.php?lang=en.
· Ip, C. (2019) *'Every Thing Every Time' Builds Poetry from the Smart City*. In: *Engadget*. Available at: https://www.engadget.com/2019/03/10/naho-matsuda-sxsw-every-thing-every-time/
· Jorge, C.; Nisi, V.; Nunes, N.; Innella, G.; Caldeira, M. & Souca, D. (2013) *Ambiguity in Design: An Airport Split-Flap Display Storytelling Installation*. In: CHI13: Changing Perspectives, Paris (27 April–2 May, 2013). Available at: https://dl.acm.org/citation.cfm?id=2468452
· Katherine Hayles, N. (2008) *Electronic Literature: New Horizons for the Literary*. Notre Dame Press.
· Krzysztof, T. (2016) *Ostatnie Pragotrony*. YouTube. Available at: https://www.youtube.com/watch?v=FIHpVf_C4wU
· Laskow, S. (2016) *Artists Are Salvaging Train Stations' Analog Departure Boards*. In: *Atlas Obscura*. Available at: https://www.atlasobscura.com/articles/artists-are-salvaging-train-stations-analog-departure-boards

· LAb[au] (2012) *signalToNoise*. Available at: https://www.lab-au.com/signaltonoise
· Mackey. (n.d.) *The Plato Clocks*. In: Flip Clock Fans. Available at. https://www.flipclockfans.com/forum/articles/9377-the-plato-clocks.
· Madeira Life. (2013) *MStoryG*. Available at: https://madeiralife.m-iti.org/?page_id=15
· Mattern, S. (2017) *Code and Clay, Data and Dirt: 5000 Years of Urban Media*. University of Minnesota Press.
· McEwen, A. & Cassimally, H. (2013) *Designing the Internet of Things*. Wiley.
· Moss, C. (2008) *BEACON (2005-2008) – Thomson and Craighead*. In: Rhizome. Available at: https://rhizome.org/editorial/2008/dec/16/beacon-2005-2008-thomson-and-craighead/
· Oat Foundry. (n.d.) *Grow with Google Split Flap*. In: Oat Foundry. Available at: https://www.oatfoundry.com/projects/grow-with-google-split-flap/
· Papp, D. (2016) *Split Flap Train Display Uses Punch Cards; Serviced with Station Ingenuity*. In: *Hackaday*. Available at: https://hackaday.com/2016/04/20/split-flap-train-display-uses-punch-cards-serviced-with-station-ingenuity/
· Penny, L. (2014) *Dearly Departures Performance Excerpts*. Vimeo. Available at: https://vimeo.com/111658408

· Raley, R. (2009a) *List(en)ing Post.* In: Ricardo, F. Ed. (2009) *Literary Art in Digital Performance: Case Studies in New Media Art and Criticism.* Bloomsbury. pp. 22–37.

· Raley, R. (2009b) *Mobile Media Poetics.* In: Proceedigns of the Digital Arts and Culture Conference, 2009, After Media: Embodiment and Context (12–15 December 2009), University of California, Irvine.

· Rinde, M. (2018) *Drexel Grads Pitch Amtrak New Sign: Vintage-Style Romance with Efficiency of New Technology.* In: *WHYY.* Available at: https://whyy.org/articles/drexel-grads-pitch-amtrak-on-new-sign-vintage-style-romance-with-efficiency-of-new-technology/

Sánchez-Calderón, G. (2010) *The Family of Man.* Available at: http://www.sanchezcalderon.com/GSC2014/Family_of_Man_.html

· Saffron, I. (2018) *Amtrak, Keep the Mod Flipboard Sign.* It's Part of Your Heritage. In: *Philadelphia Inquirer.* Available at: https://www.inquirer.com/real-estate/inga-saffron/amtrak-solari-split-flap-board-digital-20181206.html

· Schumacher, M. L. (2009) *Artist Flipping Public Projects.* In: *Journal Sentinel.* Available at: http://archive.jsonline.com/news/milwaukee/42241822.html/

· Simanowski, R. (2011) *Digital Art and Meaning: Reading Kinetic Poetry, Text Machines, Mapping Art, and Interactive Installations.* University of Minnesota Press.

· Solari Clocks. (n.d.) *Manuals.* Available at: http://solariudineclocks.xoom.it/site/index.html@page_id=189&lang=en.html

· Solari Displays and Flight YMX (2017) *Solari Schematics.* Available at:: http://solaris.concordia.ca/archives/153

· Solari Linea Design (2018) *Starbucks Open in Milan for the First Time in Italy...* [blog] Available at: http://blog.solarilineadesign.com/en/starbucks-opens-in-milan-for-the-first-time-in-italy-the-new-format-reserve-roastery-en.html

· Solari Linea Design (n.d.) *Time Keeper.* Available at: http://www.solarilineadesign.com/en/time-keeper-solari-en.html

· Solari Time (n.d.) *History.* Available at: http://www.solaritime.com/history-en.html

· Solari Udine (n.d.) *Flap Displays.* Available at: https://docplayer.net/65896487-Flap-displays-1-introduction-solari-udine-flap-displays-page-1.html: 1, 2

· Wegner, P. (2011) *Monument to Change as It Changes.* Stanford Stories. Available at: https://125.stanford.edu/monument-to-change-as-it-changes/

· Zweig, J. (2011) *Pedestrian Dramas.* Available at: https://www.janetzweig.com/public/MKE.html

Anything with a Shape Cannot Be Broken
Ian Lynam

Two items lay on the table in front of me, or more appropriately, one item and the seeming remains of another.

The item that is whole is a brand-new beige dishtowel complete with the tag from the retailer from where it was purchased and then dropped on the street for me to find, most likely the victim of falling out of the buyer's shopping bag as he or she rode their bicycle home. The tag is made of craft-colored paper and bears black, Modernist typography and maroon strips, as well as the logo of the retailer: MUJI.

The broken item is a collection of pieces of a shattered *koishiwara* dish, covered all over by repetitive stroke patterns made by the craftsperson who created the bowl. The strokes are made by deftly allowing a repurposed clock watch made of thin metal to play and bounce over the surface, creating semi-even lines of slight incisions which were then slathered over with lacquer and fired in a kiln in the Kyushu countryside along with thousands of other similar, but not exactly the same bowls. The bowl is broken because I dropped it accidentally. (As it slipped from my hands, I realized that it was my favorite piece of pottery.)

These two items could not be more dissimilar, aside from being sold by Japanese companies. Yet, that they are themselves in Japan, upon my kitchen table in Tokyo, renders any similarities seemingly moot. However, these two items have more in common than most would realize to either the domestic or foreign eye—each bears a common aura and both implicit and explicit lineage. The few centimeters of space between them is a bridge of history and of multiple, yet intertwined ideologies. The scant space between them is a story—one that is inherent in certain contemporary Japanese products, notably those fetishized by graphic designers globally, and which are the bearers of an intentionally invisible extension of Barthes' notion of "the mythological" embedded within the products themselves.

In 1957, Barthes wrote of his notion of *mythologies*—aspects of a dominant classes' worldview being espoused through a panoply of cultural products wrought by French society: through advertisements, wrestling matches, and a number of other examples. Each of the two objects before me projects a certain worldview, and that the broken bowl is bound for a pottery studio to be born again via the process of *kintsugi*, the application of gold-infused epoxy, to return the bowl to a close semblance of its former shape in only a few hours brings to mind something the potters' son once said to me, relating his parents' wisdom:

"Anything with a shape cannot be broken."

First, Mingei (or 民芸 or minshū-teki kōgei or 民衆的工芸)

The shape of the bowl was itself irregular before it dropped from my hands. It was ovoid and not perfectly round. The aforementioned patterns were imperfect. The glaze had tiny bubbles in the surface. It was purchased directly from the potter, hours north of Tokyo as declassed goods, a reject unfit for export and yet it was the perfect receptacle for countless meals in my home. As an object, it was what might be described as awkward, slightly misshapen, and perhaps even homely. The bowl encapsulated so much of what is considered to be the wabi-sabi aesthetic, the opposite of the slick and perfectly-machined, as so many popular folk crafts of Japan are.

68

That the bowl will be repaired in an irregular manner and will be made even more misshapen will imbue it with further aspects of wabi-sabi, emphasizing and highlighting the breakage. The bowl itself is what would be considered a piece of Mingei, traditional Japanese folk crafts, as like all things *Mingei*, it bore the veritable and literal marks of being made by hand, but in multiples. This mark of the hand—of being made imperfect and serially—connects the ideas of wabi-sabi and *Mingei* intrinsically.

In his books on wabi-sabi, the author Leonard Koren has incessantly argued about the aesthetics of wabi-sabi and the aesthetics of Modernism being polar opposites of each other. He is both right and wrong.

He writes in *Wabi-Sabi for Artists, Designers, Poets & Philosophers* (1995) that:

> "Wabi-sabi is expressed as though time were frozen. Objects that are considered wabi-sabi are made of materials that are visibly vulnerable to the effects of weathering as much as human treatment. Wabi-sabi objects record the sun, wind, rain, heat, and cold in a visual language of discoloration, tarnishing, rust, stains, warping, shrinking, shriveling, and cracking. The nicks, chips, bruises, scars, dents, peeling, and other forms of the notation of time passing suggest histories of use and misuse. It is because of their scarred exteriors that wabi-sabi objects have such strength of character." (Koren, 1995, p. 62)

The opposite can be said of Western modern objects—say, a Braun shaver—the hope of Modernism is to create objects which are somehow timeless and refute use and misuse.

This is largely why Jonathan Ives and the design team at Apple have so meticulously adopted the visual design language of Braun products—they are seamless and feel as though they are complete in and of themselves: objects that stand in opposition to the natural world.

It's not that easy, however, and to understand why, we need to get in our time machine and set the dial back to 1910. Additionally, we will be heading to Vienna, Austria, to observe the architectural work and writings of a popular figure at that time, notably Adolf Loos.

Everyone strapped in?

OK. 3... 2... 1!...

(cue initial blinding flash of light and the feeling of your intestines coming out your nasal cavity accompanied by one of those camera-twist-riddled superhero movie title sequences that suggests that time is a single continuum)

We queasily exit the time machine to find ourselves standing in front of the Goldman & Salatsch Building designed by Adolf Loos. This building in particular was considered radical for 1909, because the upper-half of the building was quite plain and unornamented. If we look at it, it is almost as if the building is divided in half—the bottom half is rather articulated with regard to decoration whereas the top half is largely plain. The Goldman & Salatsch building documents the emergence of notable work by Adolf Loos. It also shows how he started to make buildings less ornamental, yet had to do so first in a schizophrenic manner in order to illustrate the shift in his thinking from architectural practices and philosophies of his time.

Loos was born in 1870 and was an Austrian and Czech architect and influential writer of modern architectural theory.

When he was 23 years old, Loos traveled to the United
States and was incredibly impressed by American culture
and architecture, so much so that he described it as "Happy
America!" in regard to a country being in the total thrall of
modernity ("Ornament & Crime", 1908). When he returned
from abroad, he had decided to devote his life to architecture.
Starting in the 1900s, he designed a number of influential
businesses and buildings, while at the same time lecturing
and writing about about architecture and design.

"Less is more".
Robert Browning (1885)

   Perhaps you have heard this phrase associated with
design and architecture. It comes from a poem in 1855 that
actually has nothing to do with design, but was popularized by
the German/American architect Ludwig Mies van der Rohe in
the mid-20th century. The person who actually popularized
the notion of "less is more" was Adolf Loos. In 1910, he wrote an
influential lecture which became an essay that was published
3 years later in 1913 titled Ornament & Crime. There is one
very important part of that essay to note.

"Cultural evolution is equivalent to the removal
of Ornament from articles in daily use".
(Loos, 1913, p. 1)

   It is worth noting that Loos was just one in a lineage of
aesthetics-minded people who came to similar conclusions
about ornament. His assessment of ornamentation as being
atavistic is merely a development of the writings of Owen
Jones. In the essay "Ornament of Savage Tribes" from his
The Grammar of Ornament (1856), there are no people "in
however early a stage of civilization, with whom the desire for
ornament is not a strong instinct".

Jones went on to evaluate assorted cultures' ornamentation, evaluating them based on a British imperialist worldview.

Another predecessor of Loos was Cesare Lombroso, the "father of criminology" (Wolfgang, 1961), who posited in *The Criminal Man* (1876) that ornamentation such as tattooing was the result of genetically inherited social deviance. In the book, Lombroso presents illustrations of the tattooed bodies of Neapolitan traders, criminals, and prostitutes, using them as evidence for his theory of anthropological criminology, a cousin of phrenology. Lombroso develops the argument that ornamentation, notably of the body, but also of objects, is an act pursued only by what he termed "born criminals".

Lombroso's ideas were taken up by the Zionist writer and physician Max Nordau in *Degeneration* (1892), for the purposes of attacking what was commonly termed "degenerate art" in the German-speaking world at the time. Nordau was convinced that society itself was in a process of degeneration and that art was an influential force that helped to accelerate social, cultural, and physiological degeneration.

Sadly, a twisted version of Nordau's ideas was espoused by the National Socialist Party in the Weimar Republic during the time of the late Bauhaus, paving an aesthetic theoretical angle for racial purity and a reversion from European Modernism aesthetically, socially, and culturally, and adding proverbial wood to the fire of the soon-to-come race war.

Nordau's ideas were given their most manifest public-facing form of cultural critique by the Nazis via the traveling exhibition *Entartete Kunst* (1938), wherein over 650 artworks considered 'degenerate' were toured through 12 cities' museums in Germany and Austria.

Contemporary designers would do well to consider the twin histories of the Bauhaus and the National Socialist Party in the Weimar Republic prior to speaking of "offering design solutions" and graphic "problem solving". The flip side of this pseudo-scientific approach to speaking about what design can offer is that it is the rhetoric of genocide.

Loos' accretive ideas, incredibly influenced by Jones, Lombroso, and Nordau, about the removal of ornament were quickly picked up by designers around the world, perhaps most famously by the Bauhaus, a German school of art, design and architecture during the era of the Weimar Republic. These minimalist, function-oriented ideas and approaches to design were applied to architecture, but also to graphic design, notably by Herbert Bayer for his design of posters and typefaces, by László Moholy-Nagy for his typographic and photographic experimentation, by Josef Albers for furniture, graphic design, and countless paintings.

When we talk about "The Modern", this is what we are talking about: *utility, functionality,* and *essentialism*, at least from an European perspective.

Interlude: Multiple Modernisms

One of the difficult things about understanding Modernism when we approach the topic is knowing exactly *which* Modernism we are talking about. (The notion of multiple modernisms is something that confused me for many years when I was a student.) There are innumerable strains of Modernism associated with assorted cultures (e.g. Swiss Modernism) and sectors of cultural production (e.g. Modern British Literature), but for this essay, I will focus on three:

1. Global Modernism as a Social Project
(utopian, basic human rights, basic human needs)
1900 --> Continuing

2. Modernism in Western European
and North American Design
(utopian, functional)
1900 --> 1977

3. Modernism in Japanese Design
(largely state-driven, functional)
1900 --> 1965

Modernism took different shapes in Japan. The Meiji period (1868–1912) is largely considered the advent of "Modern Japan" with the Emperor being restored to nominal power, the government abolishing the Neo-Confucian class structure of Japanese society, rapid urbanization, and the promotion of widespread Westernization.

This period also saw the formation of Japan's modern military and the start of aggressive imperialism in which Japan would war with nations throughout Asia and Russia and annex large swaths of surrounding nations. The Japanese imperialist tendency would continue through the Taishō (1912–1926) and Shōwa (1926–1989) periods, with the goal being to create the "Greater East Asia Co-Prosperity Sphere" (大東亜共栄圏), a vast pan-Asian empire under Japanese governance and control.

Throughout the 1930s, Japanese self-perception was that of a "modern" nation, yet coupled with an increasingly militarized approach to Modernism—"the modern" of the 1930s was power, domination and occupation as much as domestic cosmopolitanism.

Were we to get back in the machine and head over to Japan around the time that Loos' work was becoming popularized in Europe, we would see that Japanese Modernism was taking form in a much different way, though the Japanese were fully aware of what is going on in regard to the development of Modernism in Europe and concerning governance, culture and aesthetics.

In 1910, Korea was annexed by Japan and became one of Japan's colonies after decades under a puppet government run by the Japanese. After the public annexation of Korea, the Japanese become very interested in its cultural output. One of these people was Yanagi Soetsu, a philosopher and fan of the arts. In 1916, Yanagi made his first trip to Korea out of curiosity about its crafts. The trip led to the establishment of the Korean Folk Crafts Museum in 1924 and the coining of the term "mingei" by Yanagi, potters Hamada Shōji (1894–1978) and Kawai Kanjirō (1890–1966). The Korean Folk Crafts Museum was a Japanese-led museum dedicated to Korean crafts, but where Korean crafts were described as having been made by "primitive, less evolved" people.

The philosophical basis of mingei is "hand-crafted art of ordinary people". Yanagi Sōetsu discovered beauty in everyday ordinary and utilitarian objects created by nameless and unknown craftsmen. According to Yanagi, utilitarian objects made by the common people are "beyond beauty and ugliness". Below are a few criteria of mingei art and crafts:

- made by anonymous crafts people
- produced by hand in quantity
- inexpensive
- used by the masses
- functional in daily life
- representative of the region in which it was produced

Along the way, the Mingei movement picked up a bunch of followers, but perhaps the most notable was Bernard Howell Leach (1887–1979), a British studio potter and art teacher who had been born in Hong Kong and lived much of his life in Asia. He spent his first three years in Japan with his father until he moved back to Hong Kong in 1890, then went to college in the UK, and in 1909 came back to Japan where he lived for a decade. Leach became very involved in the Mingei movement, writing and designing covers for Mingei-associated publications and events. As a foreigner in Japan, his involvement lent legitimacy to the Japanese-led movement and legitimized Mingei's notions of Japanese cultural supremacy.

One of the most disturbing and under-promoted aspects of Mingei was the assertion that Japanese folk crafts were superior to the folk crafts of other Asian nations. Publications associated with the Mingei movement asserted both implicitly and explicitly that the folk crafts of other Asian countries were inferior to Japanese folk crafts.

This gave rise to what some critics term "Oriental Orientalism". "Orientalism" is a term used by art historians and literary and cultural studies scholars for the imitation or depiction of aspects in the Eastern world. These depictions are usually done by writers, designers, and artists from the West.

Since the publication of Edward Said's book *Orientalism* (1978), much academic discourse has begun to use the term "Orientalism" to refer to a general patronizing Western attitude towards Middle Eastern, Asian, and North African societies. In Said's analysis, the West essentializes these societies as static and undeveloped—thereby fabricating a view of Oriental culture that can be studied, depicted, and reproduced. Implicit in this fabrication, writes Said, is the idea that Western society is developed, rational, flexible, and superior. Yet, what we find in the original mingei spirit is an Orientalist, culturally supremacist attitude toward other Asian nations and their output: an Oriental Orientalism.

This is perhaps best illustrated by a mental image I would like to ask you to conjure:

Yanagi Sōetsu proclaimed the dominance of Japanese crafts with Bernard Leach at his side, agreeing with Yanagi. Leach's foreign perspective and participation in the Mingei movement legitimized the conscious creation of "Mingei", thus legitimizing the Oriental Orientalist perspective of agents of the Japanese Empire, and de-facto legitimized Japanese imperialist thought, but through the lens of Western Orientalism.

In 1936, the Yanagi Sōetsu co-founded the Japanese Folk Crafts Museum, or Nihon Mingeikan, which is still around today and through which you can see many of these ideas expressed implicitly, but not overtly. The Mingeikan is a five-minute bicycle ride from my house and I go often. The museum's programming over the past decade-and-a-half that I have lived in Tokyo insistently and consistently highlights *the Japanese folk craftsperson as hero figure,* against a backdrop of revolving Permanent Collection exhibitions that are both historical and allude to seemingly 'savage' or atavistic aspects of the crafts output of other areas of the world. The Japanese craftsperson, be it Yunoki Samiro or Serizawa Keisuke (incidentally, an individual who occasionally dabbled in graphic design) is given center stage, while a hodge-podge mix of artefacts from outside of Japan forms the backdrop.

Yanagi Sōetsu continued to write about these ideas before World War 2, through the war, and afterward. In 1972, an English version of a compilation of his essays largely put together by Bernard Leach was published to wide acclaim titled *The Unknown Craftsman.*[1]

1 Oddly, interest in *The Unknown Craftsman* was rekindled in an eponymous article written by Richard Kenvin in the April 2017 issue of *The Surfer's Journal,* relating the crafting of surfboards to Mingei. Available at: https://www.surfersjournal. com/feature/the-unknown-craftsman/

Second, MUJI (or _____)

In the intervening years, Yanagi Sōetsu had had a son named Yanagi Sōri (1915–2011) who became one of Japan's top product designers. His works included the Butterfly Stool (1954), and the Elephant Stool, also designed in the same year. He also designed the Kettle Matte over a number of decades, arriving at the final version in the early 1990s. (My wife purchased one of these kettles for our home a number of years ago. I was unaware of its legacy at that time, though I was very aware how expensive it was.) The younger Yanagi worked in painting, architecture, industrial design, product design, environmental design, and occasionally in graphic design. Largely influenced by the writings of Le Corbusier, Yanagi Sōri was an influential Modernist who believed in the totalizing approach to design, functionalism and simplicity of unified form.

Both father and son were present for the mobilization of mingei ideologies and output used in support of the wave of nationalism and imperialist thought that became pervasive in the mid-1930s through the end of World War II through the promotion of domestic consumption and the elevation of Japan-produced products' place in the so-called "culture of daily life" 生活の文化, both in Japan and in occupied territories.

Yanagi founded his office, the Yanagi Industrial Design Institute in 1952. He designed the 1964 Olympic torch, iconic kitchenware including an award-winning tea kettle, the environmental design of the Yokohama Municipal Subway alongside graphic designer Awazu Kiyoshi, and furniture. His work bears the traces of the organic craft-forms so appreciated by his father, though extruded into mass-produced industrial form.

In 1988, Yanagi Sōri published a book called *The Philosophy of Design* where he iterated his father's notions of "The Unknown Craftsman" and applied them to modern design in an essay called "Anonymous Design". Within, Yanagi championed the products of design made collectively by unknown designers, notably:

78

- blue jeans (the predecessors to contemporary "designer jeans")
- the baseball
- the ice ax, used by winter mountain climbers

Yanagi writes about the power of the use-function of what he termed "Anonymous Design", citing the aforementioned as examples of balanced considerations of form and functionality. His writing implicitly connects his father's colonialist ideologies with global fascination with Japanese consumer products today.

Yanagi champions the rise of anonymous design and the superiority of anonymous Japanese design as marketed by the corporation MUJI (short for Mujirushi Ryōhin / 無印良品, founded in 1979 in Tokyo) in his book *The Philosophy of Design*. Yanagi explicitly mentions MUJI in the 1988 essay "Anonymous Design":

> "Recently, the Mujirushi (corporate name implying "no brand quality products stores are gaining popularity among the young. Frustrated with the inundation of brand names, the young have found peace and comfort in "anonymous design". Anonymity can truly be a refreshing antidote to the muddy whirlpool of contemporary culture today." (Yanagi, 2015, p. 14)

Most likely, as a designer, you have some sense of familiarity with MUJI and the products they sell. Despite being associated with a few leading international designers, the bulk of the design of MUJI's products are created anonymously and is in keeping with Muji's "no brand" approach to advertising and marketing.

The design vision for the MUJI brand was initially led by Creative Director Tanaka Ikko, one of Japan's leading graphic designers. (Incidentally, the late Tanaka is rumored to have been queer—something that has never been published in English or Japanese. It cracks open a giant can of worms of design history, and perhaps even more troubling that I, a foreigner *and* a straight man is outing someone posthumously. The documentation of Japanese graphic design history is completely dominated by seemingly straight men prior to the arrival of Ishioka Eiko winning the Japan Advertising Artists Club competition in 1965. That a potentially queer man was one of Japan's captains of design industry creates fissures in what appears to be a straight post-War history, rendering it not-so-straight.) Tanaka had participated in an incredible array of projects while alive—from designing aspects of the 1964 Olympics to exhibiting in *Persona* (1965), the most popular post-war exhibition of graphic design in Tokyo to working as Creative Director of Japan's largest printing conglomerate DaiNippon Printing. Tanaka designed identity systems including logos and collateral for some of Japan's largest corporations, many of which are still in use today. For MUJI, Tanaka operated as Creative Director in that he, along with Marketing Consultant Koike Kazuko and Interior Designer Sugimoto Takashi, created the entire brand vision and experience, from advertising to customer experience, to approving which products would be sold by the retail giant.

In 2001, Hara Kenya, a prolific designer and art director from the Nippon Design Center, a consortium of designers, marketers, and public relations people working with Japan's top brands, inherited the position of Creative Director for MUJI from Tanaka. (Tanaka passed away in 2002.) Hara is a prolific writer on design and has published a number of books about Japanese design—he stands as the leading design theorist and writer from Japan published in other languages in the contemporary moment. However, Hara's writing contains implicit and explicit allusions to the supremacy of Japanese aesthetics, yet when translated into English, those words are constantly and intentionally omitted.

既に出米上がった紙よりも、たった今出来上がつた紙の方がより白く感じられる。(Hara Kenya, White, 2008, p. 25)

"The paper, just finished, is far whiter than any that might be produced in the United States". [author's translation]

The above sentence has been removed from the English translation that is included in Hara's book *White*. What is being stated within implicitly is that there is a purification of craft that emanates solely from Japanese craft and design compared to American products. I find it interesting that these type of nation-state comparison-based examples are omitted in the translation, pandering to the Japanese-only reader and invisible to the English only reader of the English half of the book.

Third, a conclusion.
What is implicit, yet hidden, when one buys a MUJI product— and MUJI products are very popular with graphic designers— is the sale of specific ideologies that are intentionally obscured: various flavors of cultural supremacy and pre-war imperialism grafted onto the culture of design, much like how modernity was grafted onto a militaristic imperial governance structure shortly after Japan re-opened to the world with the Meiji Restoration.

The development of these ideologies from Mingei to MUJI was a streamlining of imperialist ideologies over generations, and much like the current Japanese government and its rollback of pacifism as defined in the post-war constitution,

MUJI seems benevolent, ready to sell you beige sheets and aluminum automatic pencils at just a tick over what would be considered "cheap".

The broken bowl I own is being repaired as I write this now. I wonder what shape it will come back in. I joked to the son of the pottery studio owners fixing it that perhaps it will somehow return in the semblance of a Panopticon, to which he replied:

"Well, Ian, as you know, the current moment
in Japan is one of fracture."

And I do know that. And I know that the centrifugal and indefatigable turnstile of tourists interested in the Japanese aesthetic will just keep coming, loading up their extra suitcases with Mingei pottery and MUJI striped shirts for their airplane trips over the Pacific. Two well-known designers I know visited recently—one from Delaware and another from Zurich. Each did exactly that. Suitcases bulging, I asked each of them why they bought the things they did.

Their answers were the same:

"It... it just looks cool."

I understand the seeming divinity of form of Japanese objects being a reflection of what one pours into a vessel emotionally and aesthetically... but when you drop one, what you see is something quite different: a thousand different visages reflecting out, distorted and misshapen funhouse mirror renderings early Modernity and of the ideologies of Loos and the denizens of the Bauhaus, but rarely followed up with that essential question:

"But what does it mean?"

Bibliography

· Koren, L. (1995) *Wabi-Sabi for Artists, Designers, Poets & Philosophers.*
· Loos, A. (1913) *Ornament & Crime.* In: *Les Cahiers d'aujourd'hui*, Paris: Éditions G. Cròc.
· Browning, R. (1885) Men and Women.
· Jones, O. (1865) Ornament of Savage Tribes. In: *The Grammar of Ornament*, p. 13–17.
Lombroso, C. (1876) *The Criminal Man/ L'uomo delinquente.* Milano.
Nordau, M. (1892/1895) Degeneration/Entartung, New York, Appleton.
· Lahuerta, J.J. (2015) *On Loos, Ornament and Crime*, Chicago, University of Chicago Press.
· Said, E. (1978) *Orientalism*, New York, Pantheon.
· Leach, B. (1972) *Tokyo, Kodansha, The Unknown Craftsman.*

· Kenvin, R. (2015) *The Surfer's Journal.* Available at: https://www.surfersjournal.com/feature/the-unknown-craftsman/
· Yanagi, S. (1988) *Anonymous Design* In: *The Philosophy of Design*, Tokyo, Yanagi Design Office, 2015.
· Hara, K. (2008) *White.* Tokyo, Cuokoron-Shinsha.
· Wolfgang, M E. (1961) *Pioneers in Criminology: Cesare Lombroso (1825-1909)*, 52 J. Crim. L. & Criminology 361.

Thanks to Chris Palmieri.

Co-Creating Empowering Economic Systems – Strategies for Action
Brave New Alps

"The economy is what we make of it."
(Slogan of the Community Economies
Research Network)

Introduction

Within the field of design, strands of critical practice have emerged that challenged the effects of the dominant economic system. But with the earth systems break-down unfolding as we write and impacting unevenly across race and gender, such a challenging mode of practice has become an imperative. Calls for change include the *First Things First Manifesto* (1964), urging designers to not be servants to consumer culture, or the newly founded *Design Justice Network* (2019), which is a more ambitious call for action. Or better, a call for revolution, namely challenging the discipline to "center people who are normally marginalized by design" in order to "seek liberation from oppressive and exploitative systems." We have personally been driven by a life-long discontent with what the dominant economic system does to us and our relations to human and more-than-human others. We have found allies amongst a trans-local group of geographers, spatial practitioners, artists and community organizers ("Community Economies Research Network," n.d.), who draw on community economies and commons approaches in order to challenge the capitalist economic system not only at a discursive but also at material and social levels.

85

This group is bound together by the desire to create more ethical economic and ecological relationships through the activation of a wide range of methodological approaches. As members of this group, we want to share the conceptual and practical approaches we draw on as Brave New Alps in our everyday design research work. We do so in the hope that others might find something inspiring and useful but also that we can critically discuss work in progress outside our own bubble of allies.

What makes a capitalist economy so destructive? The ferocious search for profit

For a long time, we had a sense that the capitalist economy in which we operate is bad for us and the planet, and that we wanted to use our design skills to critique it. However, only at the beginning of our thirties we began to more systematically look into what exactly creates the effects we considered so detrimental (Elzenbaumer, 2014). To get a grasp of the basic logics driving the capitalist economy, we spent (virtual) time with geographer David Harvey reading Karl Marx's *Capital Volume 1* (2008, 2010a) in order to understand what capital is, why it is ferociously searching for ever-growing profits and where those profits come from. The succinct definition of "capital", and thus of a capitalist economy, that we took away from this engagement and that we keep on referring to in our everyday to make sense of the world is the following:

Capital is money used to create more money. Money (M) is spent in *a commodity* (C) in order to put this commodity to use for the creation of *more money* (M'). This focus on more money, for which everything is sacrificeable as a commodity, is what makes the capitalist economy bad for us: you can have enough shoes, food, houses etc. but there is no such a thing as "enough" when it comes to money.

86

The short-hand for this logic of capital is M-C-M'. The trick in Marxist thinking – also called the *labour theory of value* – is that within a capitalist economy, labour power is also a commodity. In the M-C-M' process, the one buying *labour power and resources to be transformed* (C), has an interest in paying for them as little as possible in order to extract *as much surplus money as possible* (M') from the production process. The lower the expenses for labour power and resources (such as land, water, metals) the higher M'. In this sense, within capitalist economic systems, the ones spending the money in the first place (the capitalists) have always had an interest in cheap resources (hence no regard for more-than-human others and eco-systems) and in workers to be *free* in a perverse sense: free of access to land, housing, health care, schooling, community support, so that they have only their labour power to sell in order to make a living. This is not a natural state of being free, but a historical condition that has been produced and that is being constantly reproduced. The effect: eco-systems get destroyed and workers get worked out, while capitalists get rich. This logic also brings us straight to racism and patriarchy: when some people are perceived as less than human, they can be enslaved and oppressed, their movement restricted, their work undervalued, their habitats destroyed for resource extraction and whoever does so can still sleep at night (Yusoff, 2018).

What is there beyond a capitalist economy?
Diverse economies and commons

This capitalist dynamic is paralysing, as our everyday life and its many infrastructures are both based on this dynamic and continue to reproduce it daily. However, it is not a given, precisely because it is a complex system that has been and is being built through everyday actions. And, as designers, we know: what is built can be built differently.

In fact, sociologists Law and Urry (2004) invite us to read the economy as a performative project: the ways we conceive of the world (and with it of the economy) emerge from the world, but they also contribute to its making. This means that the economy is being made and re-made both through our actions and mental conceptions. Feminist Marxist scholars have for a long time worked on the project of performing the economy differently, both through theorising and active participation in social movements. They have persistently worked to create concepts and practices we can hold onto in the attempts of constructing economic systems based on a logic that does not destroy people and the planet for the benefit of a few but that allows the creation of just and sustainable livelihoods (see for example, Dalla Costa and James, 1971; Bennholdt-Thomsen and Mies, 1999; Federici, 2004; Fortunati, 1995; Gibson-Graham, 2006; Hossein, 2018; Biesecker et al., 2000). One approach we've found particularly inspiring and empowering is the one proposed by economic geographer J.K. Gibson-Graham, who reads the economy as *always diverse*. This means, she invites us to read our economic landscape for diversity: there are capitalist relations (M-C-M') going on, but what else? To help with such a reading for diversity in the economic activity around us, J.K. Gibson-Graham proposes to imagine the economy as an iceberg, where what is visible from above the water is the capitalist economy, while what is going on below the surface – which, in fact, is a much larger part – is the multiplicity of activities that sustain our livelihoods but don't follow a capitalist logic, such as housework, parenting, elder care, informal lending and borrowing, gifting, work in consumer and producer co-operatives, exchanges between neighbours.

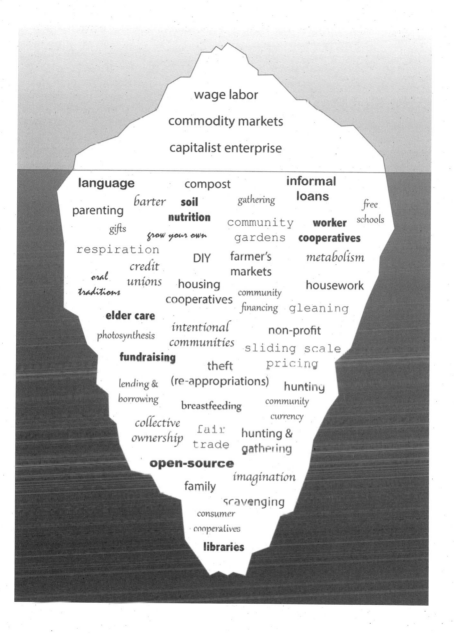

wage labor

commodity markets

capitalist enterprise

language   compost   informal loans

barter   soil   gathering   free schools

parenting

gifts   nutrition   community gardens   worker cooperatives

grow your own

respiration   DIY   farmer's markets   metabolism

credit

oral traditions   unions   housing cooperatives   community financing   housework

elder care   gleaning

photosynthesis   intentional communities   non-profit

fundraising   sliding scale pricing

theft

lending & borrowing   (re-appropriations)   hunting

breastfeeding   community currency

collective ownership   fair trade   hunting & gathering

open-source

family   imagination

scavenging

consumer cooperatives

libraries

Diverse Economies Iceberg by Community Economies Collective. Licensed under a Creative Commons Attribution-ShareAlike 4.0 International License.

While trying to understand the capitalist economy and how to change it, coming across this approach brought a big smile to our face, as it opened up possibilities – in the here and now – for imagining and co-designing economic systems that are radically different from the capitalist ones we know. So we found our design brief for the years to come: re-imagine and re-enact the economy so that it becomes an empowering and regenerative space. This moment was for ourselves a real turning point: we stopped using the design field as a reference point and instead began to position ourselves and our practice in relation to actors working towards just sustainability, regardless of their disciplinary tools. Since, we have experimented with enacting everyday economic practices that challenge capitalist logics, for example, by moving our own practice into the rural alpine space where we have grown up in. This move was driven by the desire to resist the centralising and precarising pull of capital, which lures highly educated people into cities, while also locking them into expensive ways of life that coerce them to put their time, skills and ideas at the service of projects they actually despise. In the Alps, we are now using all our energies and resources to create spaces through which people can take the social and economic matters of their lives into their own hands. We foremost do so through the co-creation of peer-to-peer learning spaces focused on practical making – such as the community academy *La Foresta* we are setting up at our local train station, an itinerant carpentry workshop activated in spaces related to refugee support systems, the community garden *comun'Orto* or the fizzy drinks endeavour *Comunità Frizzante* – as well as focusing on the activation of convivial, participatory and locally embedded research formats, such as *Il Circolo del Suolo* and the *Alpine Community Economies Lab*. Through making and researching together with our fellow local residents and our trans-local network of allies, we try to actively contribute to expand the political imagination of what the economies of our life in common can look like.

While using an eclectic mix of methods to think and enact economic systems that are inspired by the diverse economies iceberg, the commons have been another consistent reference for our design work as well as for how we organise our lives. As fellow commoner and political economist Massimo De Angelis (2007) describes them, commons and practices of commoning are material and social dimension that empower people to cultivate values and ways of relating to each other that radically differ from the ones embodied and produced by capital. We can think of commons as strategies based on a community of people negotiating access to a material and social commonwealth, where through acts of commoning they reproduce and protect a commons. This way, the commons can continue to socially and materially sustain people so that they don't have to solely rely on wage labour for generating their livelihoods. As such, De Angelis frames commons as the "conditions necessary to promote social justice, sustainability, and happy lives for all" (De Angelis, 2010).

In recent years, De Angelis has also elaborated a counter-model to M-C-M', which he calls the "commons circuit" (De Angelis, 2017, pp. 192–196), where the commons (Cs) are reproduced and maintained through commoning processes (cm).

$$\left.{}^{A}_{NC}_{C}\right\}CW\left.\right\} \ Cs \ldots cm \ldots Cs \ \left\{{}^{A}_{CW} \ \{{}^{NC}_{C}\right.$$

In this commons circuit, the commons themselves are made up of an association of commoners (A) and commonwealth (CW), referring to non-human forms of life and their ecologies, but also tools, technologies, buildings. This commonwealth splits into two different types: commonwealth that takes on a non-commodity form (NC) and commonwealth constituted by commodities that need to be acquired through the market economy (C). In other words, in this model, commons also interact with the market economy. However, a strong commons relies on non-commodity exchanges that are happening below the water line of the diverse economies iceberg for as many aspects as possible. To do so, each commons interlocks with other commons, creating what media theorist Nick Dyer-Witheford (2006) calls "the circulation of the common", where one commons sustains and feeds the other.

Within the world of designers and makers, an example for such a commons circuit and circulation is the radical printing co-operative Footprint, based in Leeds, UK (Elzenbaumer and Franz, 2018). The co-operative is hosted rent-free in the basement of a housing co-op, thus allowing them to choose who they want to provide print services for. Both Footprint and the housing co-op are part of a national network of radical co-ops that provides organisational and monetary support, but that also in turn does their print work with Footprint. Many of the printers themselves live in housing co-ops dedicated to affordable and sustainable living. Footprint generally gets its services from the co-operative sector (for example, recycled paper and phone line) or small local providers. Furthermore, each member of the co-op works only part-time in order to have time for social and ecological activism. In this commons circuit, ways of working and living are enabled that actively reconfigure and prefigure the shape of noncapitalist futures.

Strategies for linking values with value practices

In considering how to strategically co-create community economies and commons, we've also began to work with David Harvey's framework of "seven interdependent activity spheres" (Harvey, 2010b, pp. 119 139), through which he argues capital continuously evolves in its search for profit. These spheres are: mental conceptions of the world, relations to nature, social relations, reproductions of daily life and the species, institutional and administrative arrangements, production and labour processes, technologies and organisational forms. For us, this layout of seven spheres is useful when considering where to act in order to create empowering economic systems. When working on a specific project, the thinking around and designing with the seven spheres as points of orientation helps us to more systematically construct non-capitalist modes of doing and to reveal areas in our thinking and doing where we are still too much tied to a reproduction of capitalist logics. We do so by considering how every sphere is linked to certain values — either close to the logics of capital or close to the ones of the commons — that guide specific value practices, defined as "those actions and processes, as well as correspondent webs of relations, that are both predicated on a given value system and in turn (re)produce it" (De Angelis, 2007, p. 24). To this effect, we present here the working document of the categorisation we have produced so far, which is by no means complete (if it ever can be), but it serves as a tool that we can use to concretely and more systematically experiment with the creation of economic practices that activate values that capital can't accommodate. The categorisation is divided in two tables, one to outline the values and value practices that we think serve capital's M-C-M' drive, the other one to outline those we think are sustaining the creation and maintenance of commons and community economies.

Values and value practices driving the capitalist economy

Sphere	Values	Examples of value practices
Mental conceptions of the world	• We are born as individuals • Homo homini lupus • Humans stand outside nature • White able cis men are masters of the world • Endless economic growth is possible • A linear notion of time and short-sighted acting	• We learn to not identify with other humans and living beings, to activate modes of othering • The western world pretends to be "the world" and all other worlds must "develop" in its direction • The growth imperative is the economy is more important than everything else • The west refers to one notion of truth and reality and with this approach colonises the way of being, the structures of reality and ontologically occupies other territories and worlds

Sphere	Values	Examples of value practices
Relation to nature	• Nature is subordinated to humans • Separation between nature and culture	• Ecosystems and more-than-human others are resources to be exploited and destroyed for the generation of prof
Social relations	• Social relations are hierarchical • Homo economicus • White supremacy • Patriarchy • Homophobia • All sorts of ableisms	• White able cis men are framed as the masters of the universe and their desires and decisions stand above everyone else's who tend to be treated as invisible and irrelevant • It is seen as natural to try to maximize one own's profit without regard for others • Caring and sharing wealth or resources is only seen as necessary between a very close knit and heteronormative circle of people

Sphere	Values	Examples of value practices
Reproduction of daily life and the species	• Reproduction is of secondary importance to the generation of profits • Reproduction is an individual issue	• Reproductive activities are invisible, undervalued and seen as a personal rather than a collective issue • Whoever is carrying out those activities is of a lesser socio-economic position in society
Institutional and administrative arrangements	• Institutions need hierarchies to function • Private property is a cornerstone of society • Nation states and borders are necessary • Companies are equalled to people • Representative democracy is the best possible model	• Bureaucracy de-humanises people to fit into a system administered by strangers • The state is there to protect the interests of capital through police and military forces • Companies are equalled to people, capital can freely flow around the earth, while people are confined to national borders

Sphere	Values	Examples of value practices
Production and labour processes	• Production serves the creation of profits • Only work that is geared towards producing profits is valued • It is OK that some people profit while others lose out • Efficiency	• Labour is alienating and alienated: labour processes are wearing people out and the wealth produced does not end up with the people who have worked to produce it • We live to work
Technologies and organisational forms	• Technologies and organisational forms serve the creation of profits and the keeping up of social hierarchies	•Technologies are hailed as beneficial if they serve to control and subjugate people (like war and policing technologies), if they allow for the fast creation of profit (such as cheap fossil fuels, nuclear industry, computer technologies) regardless of the environmental destruction and social suffering that comes with them • Technologies perpetuate and are built with conscious and unconscious bias that keep social hierarchies around white, male, cis and able-bodied people

Values and value practices sustaining commons and community economies

Sphere	Values	Examples of value practices
Mental conceptions of the world	• All people are equal • People are collaborative beings • We are born as interdependent • Humans are part of nature • We live in a finite world • Conceptions of linear and circular time and planning ahead for several generations	• We learn to identify with other humans and living beings and are taught how to act as intrinsically interdependent • We understand the world as a pluriverse containing many different world views • The economy is about creating just livelihoods and care for the earth and people is the driving motive
Relation to nature	• Humans are part of nature • Everything is natureculture • Every species is a multispecies assemblage	• Ecosystems and more-than-human others are valued in their own right • Human activities respect and virtuously interact with ecosystems to make sure everyone can survive well together

Sphere	Values	Examples of value practices
Social relations	• All people are equal • Acknowledgement that we currently live in a world where white, male, cis, able-bodied and well-educated people have unspoken privileges	• Everyone's desires and needs are taken into consideration and made visible • People act in solidarity with each other across diversity towards a good life today and in the future • Communication is non-violent • Many instances for collective identity creation
Institutional and administrative arrangements	• Horizontal structures and distributed leadership • Private property is marginal and subordinated to commons • No nations, no borders • Enterprises are subordinated to people and more-than-human others • Consensus decision-making and participatory democracy	• People can move freely, while the movement of money is strictly monitored • Who is affected by a decision is involved in the decision-making • Institutions of the commons work to support the well-being of people and the planet • Subsidiarity is practiced with power lying at the lowest possible level

Sphere	Values	Examples of value practices
Production and labour processes	• Production serves the reproduction of life • Mental and social well-being cannot be permanently compromised through production and labour processes • We live to enjoy being alive	• Work is fulfilling and enhances people's connectivity and life energy • Dangerous, difficult and monotonous tasks – like all other – are rotated • The wealth generated through production and labour process is fairly distributed • Production serves to meet needs and capacities fairly
Technologies and organisational forms	• Technologies and organisational forms are helpful in allowing people and more-than-human others to survive well together	• Technologies and organisation forms are seen as beneficial only if they do not compromise the lives of living beings • They are designed in order to help people and the planet to thrive

What we invite you to do with this working document of ours, is to probe the categorisation we produced by using it to interrogate one specific project, design practice or mode of life through the lens of these two tables. Do the categories hold? What is still missing? What do you think is flawed? Are these categories also useful for you to develop strategies and tactics for co-creating more empowering economic models? We will be happy to hear from you.

Acknowledgements
We would like to thank Cath Muller for discussing the seven spheres with us in detail and Flora Mammana for feedback throughout the writing process. This text has been written by Bianca Elzenbaumer, Marie Sklododwska-Curie Fellow at the Center of Advanced Studies at Eurac Research (IT) and Fabio Franz, PhD candidate at the Sheffield School of Architecture (UK).

Bibliography
· Bennholdt-Thomsen, V., Mies, M., (1999) *The Subsistence Perspective: Beyond the Globalised Economy.* Zed Books, London/New York.
· Biesecker, A., Mathes, M., Schön, S., Scurrell, B. Eds. (2000) *Vorsorgendes Wirtschaften: Auf dem Weg zu einer Ökonomie des Guten Lebens,* 1st ed. USP International, Bielefeld.
· Community Economies Research Network [www Document], n.d. Available at: https://www. communityeconomies.org/about/ce-research-network-cern

· Dalla Costa, M., James, S., (1971) *Women and the Subversion of the Community* [www Document]. Available at: http://libcom.org/library/power-women-subversion-community-della-costa-selma-james
· De Angelis, M. (2017) *Omnia Sunt Communia: On the Commons and the Transformation to Postcapitalism.* Zed Books, London.
· De Angelis, M. (2010) *On the Commons: A Public Interview with Massimo De Angelis and Stavros Stavrides.* In: *E-Flux J.* June-August, pp. 1–17.

· De Angelis, M. (2007) *The Beginning of History: Value Struggles and Global Capital.* Pluto Press, London.

· Design Justice Network, (2019) *Design Justice Network Principles* [www Document]. Available at: http://designjusticenetwork.org/network-principles

· Elzenbaumer, B. (2014) *Designing Economic Cultures: Cultivating Socially and Politically Engaged Design Practices Against Procedures of Precarisation.* Goldsmiths, University of London, London.

· Elzenbaumer, B. & Franz, F. (2018) *Footprint: A Radical Workers Co-operative and Its Ecology of Mutual Support.* In: *Ephemera Theory Polit. Organ.* 18, pp. 791–804.

· Federici, S. (2004) *Caliban and the Witch: Women, the Body and Primitive Accumulation.* Autonomedia, Brooklyn, NY.

· Fortunati, L. (1995) *The Arcane of Reproduction: Housework, Prostitution, Labor and Capital.* Autonomedia, Brooklyn, N.Y.

· Garland, K. (1964) *First Things First* [www Document]. Available at: http://www.kengarland.co.uk/KG%20published%20writing/first%20things%20first/index.html

· Gibson, K. (2012) *Take Back the Economy, any Time, any Place: A Manual for Constituting Community Economies.* Presented at the Designing and transforming capitalism.

· Gibson-Graham, J.K. (2006) *The End of Capitalism (As We Knew It).* University of Minnesota Press, Minneapolis/London.

· Harvey, D. (2010a) *A Companion To Marx's Capital.* Verso, London.

· Harvey, D. (2010b) *The Enigma of Capital and The Crises of Capitalism.* Profile Books, London.

· Harvey, D. (2008) *Reading Marx's Capital - Class 1, Introduction* [www Document]. Available at: http://davidharvey.org/2008/06/marxs-capital-class-01/

· Hossein, C.S. (2018) *The Black Social Economy in The Americas Exploring Diverse Community-based Markets, Perspectives from Social Economics.* Palgrave Macmillan, New York.

· Law, J., Urry, J. (2004) *Enacting The Social.* Econ. Soc. 33, pp. 390–410.

· Yusoff, K. (2018) *A Billion Black Anthropocenes or None.* University Of Minnesota Press, Minneapolis.

Lining Out
Georgina Voss

Writing about systems is difficult and ugly. This isn't
surprising: Donella Meadows says that text alone is an
inadequate way of approaching systems.
Words and sentences must be structured

one

at

a

time

in

linear

logical

order

;

but

systems happen all at once. To engage with them properly
requires using a language that shares some of their properties.

Enter graphic design, which has been closely enmeshed with systemic concepts. I'm less interested in the specific aesthetic forms which graphical modes take. I am interested in the work that they do and their political consequences.

The very history of system – as Clifford Siskin describes it, in the singular – comes from a desire to understand and conceptualise the world, ultimately completely. This process of conceptualisation is tightly wed to what Siskin calls a 'culture of diagram'. In his astrological treatise, *Sidereus Nuncius* (1610), Galileo recorded his observations of moons moving around Jupiter through a series of delicate pictograms, sliced between paragraphs of text. The very concept of system enabled a visual epistemological shift: through seeing and using space in new ways, one could now *draw* conclusions from observations (Ong, 1956).

Modern systems theory emerges out of this concept through a deployment of the concept of 'system' to explain technological conditions of modernity. This framing is grounded in cybernetics – a grand theory of information and control in biological and mechanical systems. Developed from further sky-staring through World War II anti-aircraft research, cybernetics centres around the problem of human-machine relationships and the question of how to integrate the two into one whole system. In doing so, cybernetics intimates that systems are inherently closed and graphable, rather than messier open assemblages (Olson 2018). This urge to create controllable completeness was instrumental in the "closed world" American political imaginaries developed around Cold War military strategy.

Here,
alliances of military
and industry experts were
funnelled into national spatial control projects
to shape new forms of systems engineering in which the
world could not only be known as a universalised form
organised by function but also manageable
under the command
of a larger
purpose.

Even when stripped of militarised purpose and put to socialist use, the systemic alignment of form, function, and purpose remained. For the control room of the Chilean scheme from the early 1970s, *Project Cybersyn,* four graphic designers were hired to draw – by hand – the steady stream of flow charts and diagrams depicting national production activity. In the opening essay to this volume, Francisco Laranjo writes about how, within graphic design, the concept of systems is profoundly rooted in form and reinforced by rapid reproducibility and scale. Branding, signage, and display systems find their kin here.

A "culture of diagram" offers a simpler, more certain way of seeing the world. "I think", Donella Meadows says of using visual forms for explicating systems, "you'll understand this graphical language easily" (Meadows, 2009, p. 5). But it also creates a narrowing of vision which abstracts, away from political consequences. As James C. Scott says, "The great advantage of tunnel vision is that it brings into sharp focus certain limited aspects of an otherwise far more complex and unwieldy reality." (Scott, 1998, p.11) This simplification, in turn, makes the phenomenon at the centre of the field far more susceptible to careful management and calculation.

This raises the question: management by whom? The marrying of form and function also carries politics and intent. Consider again the design of *Project Cybersyn's* control room, which embodied structural qualities of systems dynamics, but also embedded political assumptions about who was in control. The room was modelled after a gentleman's club – low lighting, a bar where Pisco sours could be mixed – and female clerical work had all but been abolished from the space

But rewind a little. It's 1967 and the Cold War is still going strong. The second edition of Stafford Beer's *Cybernetics and Management* has just been published. Up in New York City, the first ever Consumer Electronics Show – CES – has opened its doors. Here, the sold state electronics rolling around in service of the closed world spill over into the public arena. Spread across several hotels on Sixth and Seventh avenues, CES has 200 exhibitors and 17,500 visitors who wander the sites, taking in the wonders of pocket radios and integrated circuits. The show is a success. The following year, little radios, small enough to wear on the wrist are on show; for those who want something heftier, a portable executive telephone is also on display – weighing in at 19lb, it requires an FCC licence to operate.

Technology does not sell itself, and CES is a carefully designed and managed space. At the 1969 show, Tonemaster televisions perch on tall imposing plinths which are wrapped in op art swirls. In 1971, reel-to-reel tape recorders recline on carpet-coloured platforms, dramatically lit by spotlights and surrounded by ferns. The following year, the show appears to be designed by Lego by way of Richard Scarry: a grid-system toy city of foreshortened perspective made up of ochre and blue carpeted walls, all cut through by bright red roads. Each suburb plays home to a different spectacular technology.

Colour televisions dominate the first few years of CES; later, VCRs, laserdiscs, VHS and personal computers make their way onto the carpet. Interesting shifts emerge around how emerging computational technologies are framed. CES goods are for the better part luxurious but-accessible; aspirational, future-facing, but also familiar. But computational technologies are also magical. In a *TIME Magazine* issue entitled *Computer Software: The Magic Inside The Machine* (1984), journalists describe computers as being able to 'conjure up' programs. Teenagers are framed as 'whiz kids'; technology entrepreneurs are framed as full wizards.

This is a different type of sell: one centred on charisma and heroism. Magic is about power and magical worlds are populated by heroes who are defined by presence to, and acquisition of power. Max Weber writes about how one of the key elements of magic is charisma: a certain something which endows those who have it with exceptional power and qualities: you know it when you see it; when you *feel* it. Magicians and their magical objects − in this case, personal computers − are permanently endowed with charisma. They are extraordinary, compelling.

Overwhelming reactions to modern technologies, and the men who sell them, are not new. In his work on the *technological sublime* (1994), David E. Nye describes how encountering certain types of technological forms can instil a sense of awe, or wonder, or arousal, or even horror rising up the spine. These deeply visceral feelings arise from the spectacle of confrontation with impressive objects. As Nye notes, whilst these technological forms might be large and impressive − railways, airplanes, space vehicles, even bridges − there is nothing inherently charismatic about them. Spectacle is a construct, and a lot can be done with good framing and presentation, some fireworks and song.

Whilst Nye's focus begins with a moment of reinvigorating a 'desacralised' landscape with transcendent significance at the turn of the 20th century, overwhelming and charismatic technologies – or rather, technologies which are being framed as overwhelming and charismatic – continue to seep into CES into the 21st century. Cars are the exemplar form of this shift. As fast-moving vehicles, they have the potential to be sublime; as objects packed with code, they have the potential to be magical. Since 2014, journalists at *The Verge* have pointed out that CES has been threatening to morph completely into a car show: each year, the event gets more and more car-heavy, saturated with self-driving cars, self-drifting cars, and a massive rise in 'car-connected technology (Ziegler 2014).

Technology leaders also exemplify these charismatic framings. Take Elon Musk, a man with the energy of a man who is seven double nitro brews to the wind and and very excited about his heart rate. Musk is the founder of SpaceX, a private aerospace company that's aiming for – in their terms – space colonisation; CEO of the automotive and energy company Tesla; and founder of Open AI, an artificial intelligence company. He's also smoked cannabis on podcasts; demanded dank memes on Twitter (but not moths); and, at the time of writing, embroiled in a defamation lawsuit with a British diving hero.

Musk is one of the most recognisable CEOs in the engineering and infrastructure place: whilst his public persona is a hot flaming mess, those flames catch the eye Charisma is not about niceness: people don't need to be pleasant to be compelling. The older roots of the "sublime" can refer to monstrous nightmare fuel of vast, unreal or monstrous architectures.

What are you paying attention to?

In her formative essay, *The Ethnography of Infrastructure* (1999), anthropologist Susan Leigh Star argues that many aspects of infrastructure are "singularly unexciting" and exist as some forgotten background. It takes effort to unearth dramas present in system design or restore narrative around dead lists.

Which background, though?

As writer and artist Ingrid Burrington puts it, "The language of 'invisible' and 'hidden' around network infrastructures assumes a particular situated perspective is the dominant one rather than acknowledge what certain hegemonic cultures choose not to pay attention to." (Burrington, 2019) Simplicity and tunnel vision fixates our eye to the foreground; sublime charisma keeps the eye there. All of this is amplified by the *expectation* that to engage with systems means placing that charismatic visual culture of diagram front and centre.

Ursula le Guin warns of the dangers of creating heroic stories because they set up the assumption that without a hero, there is no narrative. If technology, for example, is seen as a heroic undertaking – Herculean, Promethean, conceived as triumph (and ultimately as tragedy) – then offerings about things which aren't heroic or technological are far less interesting. Changing the hero into a *better* schematic, or a more *likeable* CEO (sorry Elon) still maintains the same structure of attention.

Heroes also make it difficult to engage with knotty systemic politics. The same issues which have shaped how certain technological forms are received as charismatic – enabled by a focus around form, branding, and marketing – also slide into their critiques. Kinjal Dave describes how political critiques of emerging technologies – algorithms, machine learning, artificial intelligence – is still focused on an individualistic critique. The terminology of 'stereotype' and 'bias' that permeate these discussions is still borne of individual perception. What these processes don't do is name or locate the systemic harms of these technologies – regulatory forms, organisational activities. Describing an algorithm as being 'biased' treats that technology as though it were a flawed person (hi, Elon) rather than an institutional force. Rather than considering the structural power of institutions, one can become captivated by the hot mess of the technologists involved.

Charismatic narratives and singular critiques generate political will for entire systems, which form-based approaches of graphic design have long been pushed into service for. In doing so, they blind the eye to the fact, to the structural politics which systems wreak. Nye argues that those who are dazzled by sublime encounters with something spectacular, are often too deeply moved to reflect on the historicity of their experience, with what feels like a unique and precious moment with reality. It's hard to think critically about something when you're enthralled in its headlights.

If we are to know systems; to parse their structural power, we must refuse simple pleasures, easy readings and compelling charismatic affect and work towards more careful attention and a more nuanced focus. Writing about systems is difficult and ugly. Moving away from heroic narratives and forms is hard. But a narrowing of vision can also be a bright spotlight; dazzling,

spectacular,

and

distracting.

Bibliography

· Burrington, I. (2019). *Twitter.* Available at: https://twitter.com/lifewinning/status/1134520166602223616

· Dave, K. (2019) *Systemic Algorithmic Harms.* In: *Data & Society.* Available at: https://datasociety.net/output/systemic-algorithmic-harms/

· Edwards, P. (1996) *The Closed World: Computers and the Politics of Discourse in Cold War America.* MIT Press.

· Laranjo, F. (2019) *Graphic Design Systems, and the Systems of Graphic Design.* In: *Modes of Criticism 5 – Design Systems.*

· June, L. & Pierce, D. (2013) *Incredible Photos from the CES Vaults: 1967–2014.* The Verge. Available at: https://www.theverge.com/2013/1/4/3828848/ces-photo-history

· Le Guin, U. (1986) *The Carrier Bag of Fiction.* Grove Press.

· Meadows, D. (2009) *Thinking in Systems: A Primer.* Routledge. Routledge.

· Nye, DE. (1994) *The American Technological Sublime.* MIT Press.

· Olson, V. (2018) *Into the Extreme: U.S. Environmental Systems and Politics Beyond Earth.* University of Minnesota Press.

· Ong, WJ. (1956) *System, Space, and Intellect in Renaissance Symbolism.* CrossCurrents 7:2.

· Scott, JC. (1998) *Seeing Like a State: How Certain Schemes to Improve the Human Condition Have Failed.* Yale University Press.

· Siskin, C. (2018) *System: The Shaping of Modern Knowledge.* MIT Press.

· Stahl, WA. (1995) *Venerating the Black Box: Magic in Media Discourse on Technology.* Science, Technology, and Human Values. 20: 2.

· Star, SL. (1999) *The Ethnography of Infrastructure.* American Behavioural Scientist 43:3.

· Weber, M. (1963) *The Sociology of Religion.* Beacon Press.

· Ziegler, C. (2014) *The Car of the Future is in Detroit and in the Desert.* In: *The Verge.* Available at: https://www.theverge.com/2014/1/14/5305072/im-in-the-desert-with-a-car

Contributors

Luiza Prado's work engages with material and visual culture through the lenses of decolonial and queer theories. She is part of the design education duo A Parede and a founding member of Decolonising Design. www.a-pare.de

Pedro Oliveira is a researcher, sound artist, and educator working in, with, and around decolonial and sonic thinking. He is one half of the design education duo A Parede and a founding member of Decolonising Design.

Belle Phromchanya's work focuses on visual research, documentary film, installation, and public events; displaying personal explorations of shifting political and social realities. In 2016, , she co-founded ACED with Noortje van Eekelen, an institute for design, art, and journalism based in Amsterdam with the aim to promote interdisciplinarity between the artistic and journalistic fields. www.aced.site

Ruben Pater is a designer at a moment in time when more design is the last thing the world needs. In search for ethical alternatives he designs, writes, and teaches. He lives and works in Amsterdam, the Netherlands. www.untold-stories.net

The **Demystification Committee** studies the intensities of late capitalism. Established in 2016, the Demystification Committee is chaired from London and Berlin. www.demystification.co

Shannon Mattern is Professor at The New School for Social Research. Her writing and teaching focus on media architectures and infrastructures and spatial epistemologies. She has written books about libraries, maps, and the history of urban intelligence, and she contributes a column to *Places Journal*. wordsinspace.net

Ian Lynam is a graphic designer and design teacher based in Tokyo, Japan. He is faculty at the MFA Program in Graphic Design at Vermont College of Fine Arts and faculty at Temple University Japan, as well as 2019 Visiting Critic at CalArts.

Brave New Alps are a design practice based in the Italian Alps. They produce participatory design projects that engage people in reconfiguring the politics of social and environmental issues. They combine design research methods with radical pedagogy, feral approaches to community economies and lots of DIY making and organising.

Georgina Voss is an artist, writer, and educator. She is a Reader in Systems and Deviance at the London College of Communication, University of the Arts London, where she is also co-founder and lead of Supra Systems Studio.

José Bártolo is a curator, educator and design critic based in Porto, Portugal. He is a Senior Curator at Casa do Design in Matosinhos, Professor at ESAD – College of Art and Design, and scientific director of esad—idea, Research in Design and Art.

Francisco Laranjo is a graphic designer and researcher. He is co-director of the design research centre Shared Institute, Porto, Portugal.